Angels are active in Puerto Vallarta

MY LIFE WITH A BROKEN WING

SHEILA ANN FRASER

We are all angels damaged in some way, if we support each other we can all fly.

 FriesenPress

Suite 300 - 990 Fort St
Victoria, BC, Canada, V8V 3K2
www.friesenpress.com

Copyright © 2016 by Sheila Ann Fraser
First Edition — 2016

All rights reserved.

No part of this publication may be reproduced in any form, or by any means, electronic or mechanical, including photocopying, recording, or any information browsing, storage, or retrieval system, without permission in writing from FriesenPress.

ISBN
978-1-4602-7980-9 (Hardcover)
978-1-4602-7981-6 (Paperback)
978-1-4602-7982-3 (eBook)

1. Biography & Autobiography, Women

Distributed to the trade by The Ingram Book Company

TABLE OF CONTENTS

Acknowledgements	v
Introduction	vii
Desiree and My New Beginning	1
Sunday Morning in Puerto Vallarta	4
Earthquake	8
A Robber at my Door	14
Banking and Buses	19
A Playgirl and Her Rottweiler	23
Meeting Isabella	28
Working in a Mexican Restaurant	31
Drugs and the Young Mexican Girl	36
Meeting Sammie and Mandi	40
My Purse Stolen Right Under my Nose	43
Dicks...to The Left	50
Wanda and the Parasailor	54
Peyote – The No No Drink	57
Canadian/Mexican Wedding	61
I'm Not What They Think	69
After 8 Invitation	73
Exotic Pet	78
Kassidy and the Shaman	82
Scorpion in Tepic	85
Tarot Readings	88
The Limon King	94
Jeff Goes to Jail	98
Mandi And The Spider	107

Some Die Too Young	111
How Star Became a Groupie	115
How to Change 100 Pesos Into 2,469.69 Pesos	118
Daniel My Shadow	124
Allan at Crystals Disco	128
Nobody Has Control with 49%	131
Crossing the Line	133
Kids on the Street	136
Canada Day in Puerto Vallarta	139
Taxi Driver Gabriel	141
Drugs in Your Drink – Watch Out	144
A Bitchslap Turns Into a Hug	147
Today's New Friend is Tomorrow's Family	152
Afterword	157

ACKNOWLEDGEMENTS

Don't be a two dimensional thinker; just because we can't see them with our eyes doesn't mean angels don't exist.

I want to dedicate this book to my father. He was and still is my Archangel. My dad taught me what was right not who, to understand the boundaries that we can cross over and the boundaries that you never let anyone cross. All my time growing up he would repeat over and over, "Family is forever, nothing breaks the circle, no matter what." Then he would follow with, "It's not the falling down, Sheila, that's important, it's the getting up that counts."

If my father did nothing else in this world he awakened *hope* in me forever. Thanks Dad, for being there always and in your acts of wisdom and with the memories we created together you are still here with me and you will never die.

To Lynda, my dearest friend for her support, guidance and influence in the making of this book. I will be forever grateful for without you this book would still be in the first stage of development. Lynda, you were my right hand, being there with understanding and literary skills. You are my Angel working always in my physical world to this very day. Thanks again, my friend.

Last but not least, to my family, friends and acquaintances that made this adventure come to be. *Gracias* and many thanks to all that came in and through my life.

INTRODUCTION

What we think we can do doesn't even come close to what is possible with angels helping us.

My Life With a Broken Wing

I thought I could fly straight with a broken wing!

This is an intro into a part of my life, my world, and some of the experiences that took place when I ended up in Puerto Vallarta, Mexico, for more than ten years.

"The truth..." I think knowing the truth is a certainty upon which many people base their lives. It gives them security and a basis from which to function. These short stories are the truth in my eyes based upon my understanding of each event and the people I am writing about. The experiences that I went through while getting my personality back into a solid, functioning state of existence, restored my ability to feel, speak, act as one. Most of the time I felt one thing and said something else. My actions didn't reflect my words or my emotions. This was not a stable place to be, *believe me!* That ability to be balanced and wanting to fly straight takes a lot of energy.

Let's begin with the fact that I was adopted. This tells you from the very start that I was born with a broken wing. The abandonment issues and the need to please others, wanting approval and needing to feel that someone loved and wanted me more than life itself always made me feel that I never quite made the grade. I always felt a little short of being the *best*.

Being a mother of three, I knew what it felt like to love another person but I never really felt that deep warm awe inside that people talked about and that knowing that someone loved me the same way. I had been told by others how they felt about me but that emptiness was still there. When I tell my children that I love them they reply with, "I know, Mom." Well, I can't do the same back! *I don't know, truly!*

I was asked once, "Who would die for you in a heartbeat?" I couldn't think of anyone. I asked my daughter, "Who would die for you in a heartbeat?" And she said in a split second... "You would, Mom."

I was astonished, "How do you know that?" I asked.

She looked at me and smiled and said, "Because you love me! That's how I know."

So there I was flying with one good wing thinking that it was normal and trying to control the uncontrollable.

I lost my restaurant due to the golf course being sold to a Hong Kong investment company. My world came crashing down around me. I decided to take some R&R with my daughter to decide my future. We closed our eyes and our fingers landed on the map, hitting a place called Puerto Vallarta. So off we went for one week.

The feeling that came over me when I landed in this quaint little fishing village was that of peace and serenity that I had no words to express. These were all new feelings that came over me. I walked around with a sensation of passion about this little town and a sense that I was home. I brushed it off and had a great vacation but that feeling followed me back to Canada and I couldn't shake it. I returned two years later with a girlfriend and it was even more powerful. While I was there I met a woman from the USA that had moved down a few years earlier. She was now my connection for my future place of residence.

A few months later, my husband decided he wanted to live in Europe when he retired and that wasn't going to work with me so we ended up divorcing. He was never ever going to Mexico again since he had not had a very good experience with the people on his previous trip. I couldn't deal with two marriages that had gone down the tubes ...blaming me of course! All the emotional turmoil and trauma of failure again...why, why, *why!* Wasn't marriage supposed to be forever? *Damn it!* So there I was flying again with one wing trying to get ahead of the game but I was spinning around and around spiralling downward out of control. That hopeless feeling of defeat was overwhelming! I made a decision to go back to Puerto Vallarta for a month to get my thoughts in perspective and a game plan for a new life!

I had holes in my soul, I was like a sieve and I needed to heal and the people in Mexico did just that for me. I will always be indebted to my dear Mexican friends that loved me for me. In time, I began to heal my broken wing and I started to fly straight, soaring to the heights of unbelievable attainment more than I could have ever imagined. I could glide and see things clearly and land without any bumps or bruising. I also got hold of my emotional fixations and my abreacting to past experiences that stopped me from letting go of my hurts and I learned to forgive and move on. I also learned that not everything was my fault and that I could only own my part. I didn't have to take the whole brunt of everyone's responsibility.

This freedom and self-control gave me an inner power that I had never experienced. Today, I know that I know that the inner awe of unconditional love is something earned not given to you, like respect, it has to be earned.

This is where the title of the book came from, I am very aware of how angels have worked in my life on a daily basis. Some people call it luck, some say, "Yeah, I was at the right place at the right time." Others call it hunches or intuition, but I call it angels at work.

Sometimes we are moved to go into a place not really knowing why but we do and the outcome is shown in our daily living and those results are the choices we have made.

We meet strangers every day and they are moved to sit beside us on buses, on planes or in stores buying groceries. Meeting others is not an accident and what we say to each other is very important. We have no idea that the words we say or the gestures we make can change lives. Yes, the angels are active always and we are never truly alone, just take the time to look around, listen and smell the roses.

These short stories are just a segment of my life and a part of my road to recovery. I hope my personality reflects my reasonable and principled thinking. A gift of oneness is what I am developing a day at a time. There are very few holes in my soul today thanks to my friends in Puerto Vallarta that gave to me without even knowing it. The power they had was by just letting me be me with no strings attached and by just accepting me as I was. They played a great part of shaping me and developing the wonderful life I have today.

DESIREE AND MY NEW BEGINNING

God, let me notice all the angels you put on my path.

—Author unknown

Desiree was the first white person I met in Puerto Vallarta. Our meeting was very unique. I had gone down to Puerto Vallarta with a girlfriend and was staying at a hotel in the Marina. One night when we were getting dressed up to go out for dinner and do some dancing at a club on the Malecón but she took ill, vomiting uncontrollably with Montezuma's revenge, not a pleasant experience that for sure. She wasn't about to venture out, so I went on my own. I had a rapport with the guys that worked at Carls from the visit before so I felt confident enough to go in alone.

I entered the place and looked around at all the tourists drinking and having Jell-O shooters, eating dinner. The music was playing loudly and groups of girls were dancing, laughing and flirting with the waiters. I spotted an empty chair at the end of the bar. I proceeded to work my way over to the spot I saw, hoping by the time I zigzagged through the crowd it would still be there. Sitting down, I ordered a drink and said hello to the waiters I knew. After receiving my bottle of Corona I started to look around the place, seeing all the young tourists having the time of their lives.

Half way through my drink a waiter named Sergio who was the perfect waiter, good looking with that beautiful smile, a body that was made from a weightlifter's magazine and his scent was to die for! He came up to me and asked if I was waiting for anyone or was I alone. I informed him of the events of the day and my sick friend and he said to me, "I have a friend at the other end of the bar that is here alone as well" and would I like to meet her. I agreed and proceeded down to the other end of the bar. I saw a woman who was as cute as a button, long brownish hair big brown eyes, and very large breasts. She was very tiny in stature. I was tall in comparison. She gave me the nicest smile.

We were introduced and I sat down and that was the beginning of a great friendship that lasted for years. Desiree could speak Spanish, which was a great help in meeting people there, she would always pretend that she couldn't speak Spanish very well as I truly couldn't.

She came to Puerto Vallarta to live permanently, having just divorced and the selling of her business and she was looking for a house to buy. With over $250,000 US in her pocket she was in a very good position to purchase a home. At that time in Puerto Vallarta, the rates in the bank were forty-four percent on a yearly rate. She was making money hand over fist. At that time the money rate was six to one. We had a great week together and arranged and exchange phone numbers and addresses.

I kept in touch with her and when my divorce came through I phoned her and went down to stay with her. She was staying at a hotel and knowing the owner my cost for staying was very, very minimal. I stayed the first time for a few months and returned home. In that time I had met a man that became my friend and he had lined up some places for me to see if I decided to take the jump and go down there for a six-month stay, which I eventually did do. Desiree had moved her mother down from the USA with her two daughters. She had purchased a home in Nuevo that was so stunning it took my breath away. I took pictures to prove to my friends on what she got for what she paid. I knew they wouldn't believe me. She was living the life of a queen that was for sure.

The last time I spoke to her she was doing very well in the timeshare business. Desiree could sell a fridge to an Eskimo, everything that woman touched turned to gold. She was amazing I could write a book on just her! Time and distance separated us and she became very involved with her daughters and her career. We saw less and less of each other, which looking back, I wish it had gone a little different. Funny isn't it, when you live next door to someone you see them every day and do many things together but with distance involved our strong friendship was tested and I guess ours wasn't strong enough to keep us together or in contact. That saying is so true, "we meet people for a reason, sometimes for a season and sometimes for a lifetime." But with time and really no other reason I lost contact with her but I understand she is in Cancun and doing well. Doing what, I don't know but I hope my friend is doing well and maybe if it's meant to be I will see her again...Here's hoping...

SUNDAY MORNING IN PUERTO VALLARTA

We are never without an angel, they are everywhere, always.

Every morning the sun comes up and it's a brand new day, the sun is shining and a soft warm wind is blowing, inviting you to start the day. You can hear dogs barking, donkeys braying and roosters crowing to each other, waking you up whether you like it or not.

Down on the Malecón, the people are walking around looking to see new things never before seen and the children are playing and laughing and the venders are on parade. The tourists are trying to cross the street wanting to get to the beach on the other side… they are waiting and waiting and waiting. The cars and buses never stop for them! Finally, maybe a tourist police officer comes along and stops the traffic, waving them on so they can cross over. I have gone shopping and the same people are still standing there patiently waiting for a break in the traffic when I go and when I return.

When you are in this land of no time and everything is tomorrow, tomorrow, you can get a little spoiled. Knowing the waiters by name and understanding how they make their living and their way of doing things, everything gets put into a different perspective and believe me is not like it is in Canada or USA. Most people work six days a week and if they are lucky get Sunday off and if they do, they are with their families: the wife and kids, mom and dad or grandparents and usually all the aforementioned. They are at the beach for the day or at church then down to the Malecón to be entertained by music or some kind of public entertainment then out to have a family dinner, and then home.

One Sunday, I am walking down the Malecón, which is a long very wide paved walkway that extends from the beginning of town all the way to the end of the hotels, which follows the shoreline where there are the beach bars and some other establishments, with venders selling their wares and many public sculptures and other scenic interests. I see a waiter with his family and I know what he has been doing all week and he gives a look of fear and terror, that *please, please don't say anything* look. I just smile and walk past as he explains my presence to his wife. The next time I see him he introduces me to them. Nothing is said and the lovely Sunday afternoon carries on.

Sunday is about the only time you see the older women of Vallarta. They shop early in the morning before anyone is up and look to the family business, banking and other family duties. The young girls work in banks and stores and go out at night to find a boyfriend and have some fun. There is not much respect for women in Mexico. The men are kings and always expect to get the best first, whether it is in education or learning the English language. The new generation of women are not like their mothers, with the accessible technology today they are rebelling and things are starting to change. They are demanding more and are standing up to the attitudes of the past.

One must get to the beach early to get the perfect spot or even a desirable spot. If the bar at the beach that you have started to call yours is open and you have been tipping well, the waiters will save you a recliner and your spot no matter how busy it gets and of course a nice tip for doing it does help for future days. If they don't like you the beachfront can be a little hectic that's for sure. With time and a good relationship with the bar they will even play your favourite music when you come in or they will play any kind of music you bring to them to play.

Sitting in my favourite place having a Corona and lime in hand, I would talk to the venders and maybe buy some fish on a stick.

When you are playing dominos, which is a passion of the Mexicans, at least in Puerto Vallarta, Mexicans that don't even speak English will come to the table and show you the right moves; at least the moves they think are correct. They watch from the corner of their eye and keep working but they yell and talk loudly and laugh at the outcome. I got my hair braided one afternoon. It had grown longer than I usually grow it. I have never braided it before but I did. I forgot I was white with very blonde hair and I got really badly sunburned on the separated parts between the braids. I have never experienced such pain. Oh my god, I was picking out dead dry skin for weeks. I could have used an angel that day!

I had forgotten about my head because I was so busy watching people doing all kinds of water sports. This particular day my son Trent had gone up and was just beginning a parachute ride when all of a sudden he stopped in mid-air and started to descend. I looked for the boat, which was quite a long ways ahead of him and it was stopped. I started to laugh. They had run out of gas and Trent was coming down, down, down in slow motion. He hit the water and the boat was just sitting there with the beach boys trying to get to him, swimming out to him as fast as they could. Fortunately, my son is a good swimmer and is very familiar with crisis situations. He had done a lot of water sports. In the meantime, another boat came to the rescue and picked him up along with the chute, back to shore they came to get gas and go again. There were many spectators on the beach that day with many comments on what had happened. Trent did state a few things of his own to the guys. Lots of harassing to the boat guys! I have seen people hit the buildings in their descent. Coming down too fast and breaking both ankles and taken back to the United States, costing over forty grand.

Apparently, the tourist was alive but that holiday was cut short that was for sure.

The sun starts to set into the horizon and you watch it hit the waterline in the distance; you leave the beach to go home to get ready for dinner and share with friends the wonderful memories of the day. You take a moment to appreciate your life and all the blessings that you have been granted, for so many have less!

EARTHQUAKE

Angels are a part of our destiny no matter what choices in life we make.

I had visited Puerto Vallarta on a short seven day holiday with my daughter Carmen six months before and had quickly fallen in love with the place. Experiencing an inner pull to this fishing village was something that had never happened to me before. The pull to return was so strong I couldn't ignore it! I wondered if it was just that touristy feeling that many people get after visiting such a wonderful place. Many say they have to go back but most don't, that feeling leaves after being at home and getting back into their everyday routes.

For me it was different. I couldn't let it go, the thoughts of being there, walking the streets, the warm wind on my face, the consciousness of peace inside me when I was standing alone on the pier at sunset that presence of awe that would surround me like a warm bath towel after stepping out of a cool swimming pool. There was a warm inner calm that engulfed me, from my head to my toes. There seemed to be a oneness with my surroundings that wasn't anyplace else. This sensitivity I embraced. I can't truly find the proper emotions to express how I felt or feel when I am there.

I went for a month staying with a new friend I had met on one my last visits. Being in a position of becoming single again, I just couldn't sit at home. Know how I felt about Puerto Vallarta? I stayed at her place for that whole month and the sensation I experienced was so wonderful and that fullness of belonging just became more and more consuming. I loved meeting the people that lived there and worked at a job on a regular basis. Getting to know the banker and store owner and calling them by their first name and they mine. While being there for one month I met a man named Morris. He was smart, kind, very soft spoken and very handsome to boot. Morris could speak English and that made it a lot easier from the beginning of our relationship. He worked for a timeshare at the Mara Hotel. Originally from Mexico City he had come to make his fortune – as many dream of doing but not too many achieve.

We communicated back and forth the months I was back in Canada and him in Puerto Vallarta. A few months had passed and I wasn't happy at home in Vancouver. I decided to go to Puerto Vallarta for six months to see how I could survive. When the time came to go down for a little while I phoned him to arrange my stay and to have him look for a few places for me to see. My son Gab had decided to come down and stay a while bringing his girlfriend …my family didn't want me to go alone; they believed the Mexican people would take advantage of me! By this they felt I would have too much empathy for the families and give them money or whatever they might need. The men in the bars would give me a sob story and I would have sympathy and could try to help them out. My sons felt I was very vulnerable never being out in the world or out in the streets so to speak. They believed I was very sheltered and would believe anything anyone said to me as if it were the truth! So Gab was chosen to come down and look after me until he was satisfied that I was going to be okay there on my own.

When I arrived it was late afternoon, a beautiful hot day with the wind slightly blowing, being also a little muggy but the smell was a little heavy …musty to the nose. When humidity is high there tends to be a mouldy scent like drying gyproc. I was feeling safe and secure upon my arrival. Morris kept his word and was there waiting for me at the airport and off we went to his place. We had small talk about the flight and me making this six-month move and discussed the apartments that we would be looking at. We went to dinner and had a very lovely evening. This was October the seventh. On the morning of the eighth, Morris went to work letting me know he would be back by noon to go to the airport to get my son and then off we would go apartment hunting.

Well! I was lying in bed wondering if I had done the right thing in moving down here for six months. You know all the things that pop into one's head ... the do's and don'ts, should and shouldn't, assuring myself I made the right decision. And I could change my mind, since nothing is ever written in stone. With these thoughts going through my head the bed started to shake. I looked at the walls and they were moving in and out in slow motion. I thought I was in a horror movie with those walls curving and moving. Everything started to vibrate – the water glass started to move, wiggling across the table, splashing water all over the table top and fell off the night table falling to the marble floor, smashing into a million pieces. The painting on the wall started to sway, moving back and forth like it was trying to get off the hook. Which it finally did as it came crashing to the floor. When I looked up, the ceiling fixtures were swaying as if a strong wind had gotten into the room.

My mind was going a mile a minute and I thought, *Oh my god it's an earthquake!* I had never been in an earthquake before and it was terrifying. I found myself to be much disorientated and my equilibrium was out of sync. I felt so strange and I tried to get my thinking in proper perspective and do something. Trying to get dressed was an ordeal with everything moving and trying to get my balance just to put my jeans on was an experience on its own. It was difficult to concentrate on what was happening to me with hearing people yelling in Spanish, dogs barking, kids crying, cars honking their horns.

My thoughts of the building of five stories coming down and crashing on me, being on the first floor but that being one flight up, I was thinking about my family...hundreds of things rush through your mind in an instant. It's like time stands still and a lot of time has passed but it's only seconds in reality. I finally got dressed and then the tremors stopped ...just like that! I rushed out of the apartment and down the hall and down the stairs and out to the street. I witnessed chaos everywhere...nobody seemed to be hurt and no buildings were down but there was turmoil every place I looked. I wasn't scared just a little confused at my next step. I was shaking only because I think I had the wanting to flee but didn't know where to flee to. And what should I do first? People were coming up to me saying things in Spanish I didn't understand. They were making the sign of the cross over their chests. Buses stopped all over the road with people getting off and going this way and that. I took a deep breath and thought, *I have to phone home!*

Up the street a few blocks away I saw a phone booth and went to call home. In the process of getting to the phone I looked up hearing my name being called and it was Morris white as a ghost with fear in his black, black eyes. Grabbing me and talking so fast in English I could hardly understand, he proceeded to tell me his experience, of where he was and what he was doing at the time. And there would be several more tremors throughout the day and to not be frightened. I eventually phoned home to be greeted by my daughter crying and with sounds of relief and tears of joy (at least I hope they were) letting my children know I was fine and that her brother was still in the air and hadn't landed yet but didn't know the state of the airport.

Morris had said that the most famous church – Guadalupe in the town center – that its Crown had fallen off but nobody had been hurt. They replaced the crown with a fake copy for quite a long time. I couldn't be exact on this timeframe but the original took a while to be fixed and put back, in the meantime everyone that had lighters with the church on it or pictures took the time to white out the crown till it was restored and put back.

We went and picked up my son at the airport, which I might add was a little hectic. There were so many people and more cars than usual. Just trying to find them in the very crowded terminal was time-consuming indeed. But, once I saw him behind the fenced area waiting to come to me I had a sense of relief they knew nothing of what had occurred till it was time to land and they were informed of the event that had just happened but all was well but they might have to circle for a while.

After all that excitement we still got ourselves together and dropped their luggage off at Morris' place and got our plan for the day under way.

We went to have lunch and discuss the day's events and went to look for places – five in all. The first one was awful, just unthinkable for us, the place looked like a kid had built it, there were wires hanging everywhere and in the bathroom area the toilet faced the wall that had a shower nozzle hanging (sort of,) pointing at the toilet where you could literally shit, shower and shave! The water from the shower just fell to the ground and ran into a hole under the sink! No lip to catch the water from going into the hall of the apartment. It was so funny to us we had a great laugh and quickly went to the next. The second was up about fifty or more steps to the place from the street...that was a *no!* I wasn't hiking to my home that was for sure!

The third apartment was up the mountain looking down on Vallarta, the view was beautiful but too high up. It would take forever to get up and down the path. Nice, but to get to a taxi or to the road was too much work for me. But the fourth was perfect so we never did look at the fifth one.

This place was in Old Town, which they call the Romantic Zone. It was a three story building, which I found out later had a few Canadians living full time there. Our apartment was on the second floor just one flight up facing the road with a large balcony. It had three bedrooms, two bathrooms with showers only but separate from the toilet area. They both had lovely sink tops and cabinets below. Glass doors on the shower areas. Nice kitchen, bad fridge and stove not so hot but okay. A back room so big you could have a party in it and never need any other space.

The hall entrance once inside was spacious as well. Looking off the balcony you could see the hospital on the corner up the street, the bus stop was on our corner and half a block away the taxi stand had taxis there all the time night and day. From our balcony, Gab would whistle and they would look up and bring the cab to the door. It was one block away from restaurant row where there were at lease twenty different kinds of stores from pizza places to a bakery to a grocery store. It was perfect and I stayed there for over ten years and never did move from my six-month adventure. My son and his girlfriend finally left with a feeling of a little disappointment on his part. He tried to teach me Spanish by labelling everything but seeing that that wasn't going to work he gave up and shook his head and smiled and said to me, "I tried, Mom ...*you're on your own!*

A ROBBER AT MY DOOR

By choosing a higher path it's possible to soar like an angel, by choosing a lower path, it's possible to become a worker for evil.

One evening we decided to go out for dinner and do some dancing. My son's girlfriend had come down to Puerto Vallarta for a few months. She was a model in Europe and had decided to take a few months of R&R with us.

We were on our way home from a wonderful evening discussing how quiet the streets were because it was the end of the week for many tourists. The ships would be arriving in the morning with new tourists and the planes coming in would be taking the last group of tourists back home.

As we walked leisurely along the road taking in the warm evening on our adventure, showing Dianna our local haunts, we looked towards our apartment and out of our doorway we saw a stranger wander out. This was very out of place. We looked at each other and wondered what was up. He was walking quite fast; it was too late for visitors. All the lights were out and the building was in darkness.

My son looked at me and began to jog ahead of us. Within a few minutes we were at the sidewalk in front of our place and my son came running past us yelling, "That son of a bitch was trying to rob us!" Up the street ran my son in the direction that the stranger went, Dianna in pursuit. Near our home was a short street that leads to the main highway. Along the street were parked cars, bushes and trees on the right and on the left were two or more homes and around the corner some stores. I watched Gab chase the guy and he dove under a car parked on the side of the road. Gab went to the other side of the car and the thief rolled out the driver's side, got up and started to bolt around the corner. Dianna was now almost at the car where this was all taking place. Gab ran in front of the car and disappeared around the corner, out of sight, with Dianna following close behind.

I ran up the one flight of stairs to our apartment door to find wood chips all over the hall floor, and the lock to the door almost jimmied off!

I was by then running down the stairs yelling at the top of my lungs,"*Ayudarme...Ayudarme!*" (which means help in Spanish, one of the few words I do know). As I was screaming and waving my arms, a young man came running up the street towards me. Like an angel dropped out of the sky! He asked me in English what was wrong, and what happened. I proceeded to tell him and when I was half finished my sentence, he took off up the street in the same direction as Gab and Dianna. I found out later he was on his way home from visiting friends; that he works in Alaska and was staying with his family for a few days. Raphael was originally from Mexico City.

I could hear Gab yelling and swearing and I looked up the street and spotted Dianna crying and screaming. As she got closer I saw blood running down her face. It appeared to be coming from her eye or very close to it!

Everything was happening so fast I could hardly comprehend what was going on. Now the Tourist police were by my side, two men and one woman dressed in white uniforms. They were looking to Dianna's face where it was cut open and would probably leave quite a scar, which is very, very horrendous for her, in her line of work. She was very devastated!

As all this was happening, two huge white police trucks arrived with two officers in navy blue uniforms carrying warlike walkie-talkies or some kind of radio devices in each truck. Dianna told them that the robber went around the corner and tried to stab Gab with some kind of weapon and Gab ducked, and the thief missed him then threw it at him. It missed but it struck Dianna in the face and bounced somewhere into the bushes nearby.

The *Federales* in black uniforms then arrived in their jet black trucks and holding really big black guns. Off they went to find Gab and Raphael and hopefully, the robber.

The local police told me to get in the truck with them. I did and off we went in pursuit, in the opposite direction. With lights flashing, talking into their radios a mile a minute...and me between them not understanding a single word, we were going so fast up and down the streets. We passed the *Federales* at one point and I saw my son and Raphael in the back of one of the trucks holding on to the roll bars and yelling something and pointing madly at some area beside the road.

We had been driving around and around for quite a while, at least it felt like that. I saw streets and rivers I have never seen before, it was quite a tour. Then all of a sudden we got called to the bridge and when we got there we were stationed at one end of the bridge, the *Federales* at the other. The police officer told me to wait in the truck and not to move because they didn't want this thief to see me. "If he is let go, he will find you and hurt you," they said. My back went up and I wanted to get this crook, nobody is going to threaten me and my family. I would rather die fighting than live a life of fear!

The four police officers left their trucks and went to the other end of the bridge where the others including my son were gathered. I couldn't see what was going on but I found out later that the thief was in the back of the truck with my son. The *Federales* asked my son what he wanted to do with the thief. Gab said, "I will charge him and put him away!"

The police didn't believe us and Miguel told them in Spanish that it was true, that we would lay charges and follow through. They were very hesitant because they really didn't believe we would follow through, but Miguel convinced them we would so they started the paper work.

In the meantime, they were getting statements from Gab and Dianna. After the paper work was completed they took Gab with them to search for the weapon. The local police were looking for the weapon as well and within an hour they found the weapon in the bushes. It was a screwdriver. In the meantime, the tourist policewoman had taken Dianna to the hospital to have her wound seen to. They were wonderful, they never left her side.

The thief was Jamaican and had been robbing people in the neighbourhood and threatening them by swearing that if they reported him he would be back to hurt their family.

Gab couldn't say for sure if the screwdriver they found was the exact weapon but apparently it was good enough. Gab was so furious with the whole affair he told the officers that we Canadians may be compassionate and polite but nobody messes with their family...*ever*!

The next morning they came and got my family and took us to the police station in town to review their statements from the night before and within a week we were in the court house. The Jamaican was charged with attempted robbery, assault with a deadly weapon and attempted murder and when all was done, he was deported and never allowed in Mexico again.

Apparently, the government aided us in the procedure and the newspapers had written about the incident on how a Canadian family had been assaulted and had laid charges. Justice was served. My friends told us about the article, as I was unable to read Spanish myself.

After that, every time I passed a police officer they would nod and smile or wave. It was so nice to know that I could walk the streets and feel safe. So you never know from one minute to the next what's going to happen. After that chaotic night we never did see Raphael again to thank him for his help. Once again, I think it was evident that Angels are very active in Mexico.

BANKING AND BUSES

*Staying in the "Now" allows us to see
what the angels want us to notice.*

When you live in Puerto Vallarta it takes you a while to understand how things work... you must understand how it works to have things run smoothly. You learn a little at a time from your experiences as the days go by. When you walk down the street and talk to the local people at work you greet them with a hug and *hola*. These are basic if they don't understand English and as the conversation expands a little more it becomes a language of hand gestures and facial expressions. Once you do understand Spanish a little it becomes much easier.

I chuckle when I think of how my hands and my Spanglish got me by and amazingly, they understood me most of the time. I would walk to Ravens, the local grocery and department store, to get my groceries and have a wonderful time. Sometimes, if I had a lot of groceries I would pay the young man who packed them for me twenty pesos to carry them home for me, which was about five long blocks away. They were actually allowed to just leave and go with me to my home and it was great. I would rather give them the twenty pesos than pay for a cab.

The funny thing about the Spanish and the English is if you are English speaking you have a tendency to talk very loud and slow. (Whatever makes us think that by doing this they can understand you better ...ha-ha but we do!) The Spanish speaking only take your hand or arm and guide you to the thing you want and point at it. Like they think by doing this you will understand. It is funny to watch this happen and I found it very entertaining indeed, even more so when they did it to me.

As you go about your daily chores it helps to be in a good mood and have a lot of patience. I would go to the bank for instance and that was a day long procedure if you knew someone in the bank, which I did. They would whiz you through maybe, but if you didn't and you didn't know the system, you could forget being in any kind of hurry as you could be there all day and they really don't care. I have stood in a line only to find out at the end it was the wrong line and away I had to go and start all over again.

If you're lucky it's a bank where you take a number to be served and that way it does go faster. I remember going with my girlfriend Lynda to get some money that had been wired down to me. We went to pick up the monies. The place was at a furniture store... go figure. We went with my birth certificate, address of my residence, passport, etc, etc. ...if you knew the people running the establishment no problem but if you were a stranger and it was your first time, that was a different story.

We were in line standing and wait, wait, wait. We were there for half an hour with the girl behind the glass wall doing nothing... really, she was just sitting there doing squat, just sitting there looking around talking to one of the salesmen. It was very frustrating and she would look over then she would stroll past and look at us... "No hablo English" she would say and smile, I would reply, "*No Español.*" She would shrug her shoulders and look at us till we finally got through to her what we wanted. I would laugh and laugh. To me it was fun trying to communicate and trying to write things down or draw something. We finally were able to get through to her what we wanted and she went and got the papers to sign. Everything was complete. She went to get the money and put it on the counter about ten inches out of my reach behind the glass, she then proceeded to pick up her purse, looked at her watch and left. We looked at each other as she locked her cage and walked out. Was she done for the day? Done and she left the building! We looked at each other and just stood there.

Then we got the attention of one of the salesmen who spoke a little English and asked where she went. He told us she went for her lunch and would be back in two hours. I was so shocked all I could do was laugh. We told them that it was my money behind the glass window and I wanted it and he said he didn't have the key and I would have to wait. Now I was getting mad and so he went to get the manager. The manager told us to calm down and he would get another person to get it for me. And about fifteen minutes later along came another girl, she looked at me, got into the cage and looked around. Then she left then came back to the cage and pushed the money out through the hole and said, *"Adios señorita," and* she left. Amazing!

As we left with a feeling of absolute frustration we shook our heads and once again laughed because there is nothing else you could do. You are at their mercy unless you take a Mexican with you and then it's a whole different situation indeed. Now we had to go to the bank. When you are going to the bank you have to cross the street at one point and to do so you must believe in God or you must think you are blessed because if you don't just step out you will never get across... we ran across the street and went to the bank to get some money from Canada and you have to understand the workings of the ATM in Puerto Vallarta. They function from two trunks, one from Mexico City and one from Guadalajara. If you go to one bank and nothing happens, you don't receive your funds. You must go to another and another. Them not working or out of money doesn't mean anything. It could be that the trunk is down but if you go to the bank and you hear a little rumbling noise in the machine it's a sign that you are going to get your money you know it's coming it's just a matter of a few minutes, but no little noise means no money. You tend to hold your breath and stand there and wait for the sound and if it comes you feel like you just won the lottery.

Riding the bus is another experience in itself. There are different coloured buses for each area and those colours you better get to know real fast! Black and white ones, blue and white, white and green, and white and orange. When you ride the buses you get off and on when you want. You can flag them down and they will come to a stop. Well, sort of a stop; and then away they go. You have your money ready and you jump on and off, if nobody is around, but there are official stops where they have to stop if there is anyone there or someone wants off.

The buses pass each other like they are in a race. Between legal stops you're on your own and if they like you they will stop and wink at you and let you off but if they don't you can just forget it. A legal stop is the legal stop even if its blocks away from where you want to go. The buses are not company owned. Every driver owns his own bus, to my understanding, and they have a specific route. How they get it, I don't know but that is why they go so fast from stop to stop. Every fare counts and they get paid per ticket. There are spotters that get on the bus from time to time to make sure you have your ticket handy to prove you have paid.

Some buses are painted really nice with chrome exhaust stacks, bumpers and grills and wheels with chrome covers. They look really nice. Some I wouldn't even get on have broken windows, all rusty, graffiti scribbled all over. The younger drivers have newer buses and most of them today are quite nice. The young drivers love their buses and dress them up like the kids do with their cars. The more chrome the better! They are really clean inside and out. So that was our day, shopping, bank, bus, ATM and home. By the time it was finished it was five o'clock and having left around nine, it had been a long, long day to do something that in Canada would have taken maybe an hour. But that's Mexico, and I really could have used an angel in my corner that day.

A PLAYGIRL AND HER ROTTWEILER

Guardian Angels though we can't see them are always watching over us.

One night I was all alone at a bar about three blocks away from my home. It was a bar at night and a wonderful restaurant by day called The Twin Parrots. The atmosphere in the place was friendly and I always felt I could go by myself feeling quite safe and secure that nothing bad would occur there. I was sitting having a nice cold drink and needing to cool down from the hot wind that had been blowing through town all that day and continued into the night. I was hoping that it would get a little cooler before I went to bed.

I looked around and I saw a beautiful girl sitting by herself and not looking too happy. She had the saddest face and when she looked at me, I just couldn't resist calling her over to join me. Well, Tara was a single mom living with her daughter and her famous ex-husband was paying her a lot of money and her divorce was just going through… She didn't want the divorce and this very distant separation from her home in the United States was overwhelming her. She told me that she had been a playboy bunny at the Mansion and life had treated her well till her marriage broke apart.

She told me her story and as she was telling me I couldn't help but think, "*Wow, money, glamour and now this?*"

We talked till the wee hours of the morning... she had been there for only a few months but had not really met anyone.

We agreed to meet the next day for brunch and when we did she asked me to come to her home and meet her daughter. *Oh, my god!* Her place was a villa! Tara had a brand new red jeep in the driveway that was inside the huge wooden gates that surrounded her entire property. I felt like the poor little church mouse. I walked into her place through front doors that were so high you would need a very large extended ladder to get to the top. You could get a nosebleed. The sitting area was as big as my front room and contained living trees and plants with a very expensive chair and a loveseat and side table. From there we wandered to the open area that was shaped like a U with a massive swimming pool in the middle, around the U-shaped area there were many doors, one for kitchen that was so high tech it looked like it came out of a magazine. The other rooms were custom built as well. As I walked around, I was trying to keep my mouth from falling open and repeating the one word: *Wow! Wow!* One room had a pool table and all the little goodies that go in that kind of room: corner bar with fridge and stools to sit on while playing pool or other parlor games that were open and on display ready to play with. An open bar area to sit at by the pool but under cover just in case it should rain...LOL four guest rooms, which she said I could choose one of them and I could move in today if I wished and I could have it forever if I wanted. Or if I wanted to move in and just stay, it could be for as long as I chose. One opening was the dining room with a grand piano off to the side and special coverings on the wall pictures that were on display behind the baby grand with the perfect side tables and décor that suited the room to a tee from the perfect coloured wall to the curtains that draped to the side of the window allowing you to see the ocean beyond the balcony. Tara's bedroom and her daughters' were around to the side away from the other rooms and very private.

These two rooms were just as stunning. I just looked at her and couldn't for the life of me wonder what the problem could possibly be. If your life is good then money makes it even better but I guess having an awesome house means nothing if you feel like you have no self-worth. To want for nothing materially has never been in my blueprint. Happy but poor I guess in her eyes, but I think if you are happy a little extra doesn't hurt.

As I was walking around this fairytale mansion I heard the loudest bark I have ever heard in my life. I just froze and thought okay! Life is over...I turned and the biggest black and brown Rottweiler was coming at me. Huge! I mean *huge!* ...scared me half to death. Tara started yelling her name: "Cindra, Cindra ... *stop!* Come here!"

Well that didn't do much good... she wasn't listening to her owner. This massive dog stopped in front of me, sniffed me and started to lick my hand and arm in one fell swoop ...lick...lick almost knocking me over in the process.

Tara started laughing saying she couldn't believe it, "Cindra doesn't like anyone ...oh my goodness...this is great!"

I am standing there thinking, *Yeah! Her head is bigger than mine. She could eat me like a cookie! And still be hungry!* In a few minutes, which seemed like an eternity, all was good. Cindra settled down and wouldn't leave my side. She even followed me to the bathroom, which after that experience I needed! Not sure which end I was going to release first. The main bathroom took me extra time for I had to look at the décor in that *baño*, it was out of a picture book.

The home was American built not sure who the builder was but it was *fabulous!* Just walking through it was a fairytale.

Her daughter was a little precocious but no kidding! Little Miss Princess with an attitude!

Back to this dog! Every time I went there for coffee or she would come to my place that darn dog was there. It would fall down at my feet and just stretch out and lay there. If my feet were under her I didn't have a chance in hell to move. One night I was walking down to the Malecón and I met her on the street walking this beast and Cindra smelled me or spotted me and started to bark and jump. She took off like a bullet straight towards me but by then I could tell her what to do and she would obey my commands even though she still didn't really listen to Tara! The chain that she used to hold her was huge that's for sure, and the collar was like a big belt with studs on it ...that dog was scary. She stood beside me and her back was at my waist and her shoulders, neck and face came up to my chest. She had been a champion at one time...she had trophies everywhere. She probably coaxed the trophy out of the judges by being just plain scary. She was beautiful really, a beautiful show dog, once you got past her size and the fear of being eaten she was so sweet.

Before we got to the Malecón, Tara asked me to do her a big, big favour... "Would you walk the dog to the other end of the Malecón and I will meet you there..." She had to do something and she had to do it alone. I said, "You've got to be *kidding*, you want me to take this beast on a walk alone on the Malecón! If she ever got away from me I wouldn't know what to do, she could literally drag me along behind her and whatever she was after would be dead too!"

She begged me and I said, "Okay, but don't be long! So she gave me the doggy and lead chain and off she went.

My goodness, we started off on the Malecón and it was a Friday night so you could imagine the crowd of people walking and taking pictures, buying from the venders and talking to artists on the side of the road. Kids with balloons and candy floss.

As we passed everyone, I looked into Cindra's eyes and said, "You be good *or else!* Whatever that could possibly mean. So we start off. She was wonderful strutting right beside me. Walking by my side looking straight but close to me, she acted as if she was proud to be protecting me. People were giving me comments like... "Oh my god, look at that dog, she is so small how can that woman have the power to hold her?"

"Ha-ha," someone yelled, "there goes Harley and her Davidson." Others asked me to stop and let them take a picture of us.

When we walked along, it was like a path opened up for us, we didn't have to make way or go around anything or anyone. Waiters were whistling off the restaurant balconies at me. There was a point half-way down the Malecón where I ran into a couple of friends and we stopped to talk and Cindra got tired of standing by me so she just plunked herself down right on my feet and sat or laid there till I was done and then she got up when I told her to and off we went. We arrived at the end of the Malecón and Tara was there a few minutes later thank God and we walked back to Old Town which is called the romantic zone and of course we passed Foxy's and it was a-hopping and Tara wanted to go in. I said, "Right! With the *dog?*"

She said, "Why not, I will pay to have her in a special VIP section and get someone to hold her collar while we dance!" We went up the street and got some spareribs (beef ribs of course) so Cindra could have a snack while we drank and danced. So when we got to Foxy's they said "no dogs allowed" especially that one! Tara paid the door man a hundred bucks and away we went to the VIP section and hired a guy to watch the dog while we danced and had fun for a couple of hours. We left, thanking everyone and then they were thanking *us*, ha-ha, no kidding they made more money in two hours than they did all week.

So now we are tired and try to get a cab but it didn't matter how much she offered them nobody would take the chance on having Cindra in the back of the taxi…and two drunken women… so we walked home. It took forever but we made it.

I had several more months with Cindra taking her for walks alone on their private beach and playing catch with her and throwing a stick into the water for her to fetch.

She was a great dog and I have about a year of wonderful memories. One year later, she had a tumour and died. She was a great dog that's for sure. R.I.P Cindra. You were a four-legged angel in my life. I will never forget you. Wherever your doggie soul went my friend, I hope to see you again in the next realm. God willing.

MEETING ISABELLA

*A material gift is never a substitute for
the gift of an awakened heart.*

My friend Michael, with whom I am still friends today, asked me to read his cards, so I did. After I had read his cards, he left suddenly, without explanation. It seemed a little strange and I wondered what I had done, if anything. A couple of days later he arrived at my door and proceeded to tell me there was someone he wanted me to meet, her name was Isabella. She was a psychic and he told me that when I read his cards I had said almost word for word what she had just told him! I looked at him and smiled.

He said, "She wants you to read her cards. In all the years she has done reading nobody has ever said the same exact things."

I said I couldn't read her cards. I wasn't a professional and I don't think I could do a good job.

He just laughed and said, "Yes, you will." We decided to meet and exchange readings … well, that didn't work out for a couple of weeks and when we did find the time, she came to my place.

A knock on the door and there she was…and she wasn't what I pictured at all. She was a tall woman in her early forties I would say, white and from Canada. Vancouver actually, she was what they call an OPC she worked for timeshare and was very good at it apparently… she made a lot of money… you are good at it or you are not and if you were good, like her, the money is great.

She came inside and sat down. After a few minutes of chitchat, I gave the cards to her to shuffle and believe me, I was very nervous, my mouth was dry and I thought, *Oh God, please help me to do a good reading.* As she passed the cards back to me I started to shake …I looked at her and said, "Are you nervous?" and she looked at me, looked to the floor and said, "Yes, I am!"

All of a sudden the energy shifted and I was calm and I knew I had the upper hand. I was in control. I thanked God in silence and went on with the reading. To be very honest at this point I really didn't remember anything I told her, it all came out then all of a sudden I had nothing more to say, very strange. That was that. She paid me because she said money crossing the table was very essential. The amount wasn't important but it was making the reading valuable.

She came back a few days later wanting another reading. I asked, "*Why?* Was the reading off, or what?"

"Are you *kidding?*" she said, "It was so on the mark that I need *more!*" And from that point on she would come every three or four days for a reading and she would laugh and say she was working to pay me! I could read her so openly and so quickly it was scary. I don't know how I did it or how it truly happens but I say what I feel or see in my mind's eye and when there is nothing more to say I am finished.

I hadn't asked her to read me until one day she called to come over and I wasn't feeling well. My stomach was hurting badly and I truly didn't know what the hell was wrong with me. As I was telling her she stopped me and began to talk really fast. She started with, "Oh, dear you have to phone home and you have to do it right away." She said, "Something is wrong with your family, it's about a little female, oh dear …please phone when we hang up!"

So I did, I phoned home to my son to see who the little female was.

He answered the phone and in an instant I said, "Okay Jeff, what's wrong?" He started to cry and told me that my granddaughter had Bell's Palsy and they didn't know what was going to happen, that her little face was paralyzed on the left side, her eye was partly closed and her lip was drooping and she had been put on steroids. They didn't want to tell me because I was so far away. Well, far away or not I was on the first flight out of town! Isabella came over and so did Michael and we talked about it as I calmed down and packed.

Isabella was so taken with my readings, which were very different from hers, that it seemed fascinating to her. She would send people over to me all the time and would tell them how much I charged and they paid and apparently left happy. She always did a follow up with the clients being in the business she was in. I became very close to her and we saw each other at least three times a week until I went back to Canada and we lost touch. I have no idea where she is today. I hope she is together with her children in Canada. I hope one day we will run into each other at a mall or store in Vancouver. I have no idea where she is and I have no way of contacting her. I do know her angels are watching over her and working with her to resolve some family issues. I wish you well, my friend.

WORKING IN A MEXICAN RESTAURANT

If we pay attention to our instincts, intuition, and ideas the guidance of the angels will become real for us, not just a fantasy.

My son Gab and I were walking along one of the side streets on a warm and windy Sunday afternoon wondering what we were going to do with the time we had here in Vallarta. My son came down to stay with me for a while because my other kids felt that I needed looking after. Jeff, one of my sons, felt I needed protection from the Mexican people. He felt that they would take advantage of my kindness and empathy for them and I would give every material thing I owned away to help them solve their problems. They always had a lot of problems to solve!

I couldn't understand his concern since I raised him on my own and I think I taught all my children the basics of life and how to take care of themselves. I believe the apple doesn't fall far from the tree so didn't see the problem. Gab was there until my oldest son was satisfied that I was safe or Gab got bored with being there, whichever came first. After a while if you are an active person you can get bored there. I have always been the kind of person who had some kind of goal or something in the works to stimulate my senses. At this point in time, Gab and I had nothing going on.

Walking and just talking about the future we ran into a very dear friend Renato whom I met a long time ago in Vallarta. He had visited my home in British Columbia where he and Gab met and we all got along really well together. We found out through our conversation that he was having trouble getting anyone to work for him. He needed a hostess and a bartender for the two weeks leading up to Christmas and over New Years. Gab looked at me and smiled and I looked back and said, "Sure, we'll help you over the holiday season." We agreed to go in and get familiar with the restaurant layout, the menu, and he also agreed to show Gab the ropes in the bartending world.

Now to begin with, you have to understand that people get paid, on the average, around fifty pesos a shift plus tips or, they just get paid by tips. They work nine to twelve hours a shift. As a hostess, I wouldn't get paid but I would get a percentage of the tips received. Gab, as a bartender, would get fifty pesos a day plus a share of the pooled tips. My son started a week before he was really needed, to learn how to tend bar and I was to go in for a couple of shifts before Christmas week.

The place was very busy and it was long hours but it was great. I loved talking to the tourists and hearing where they came from and why they were there. I just can't get over the way they dress...I know it's not very nice of me but why do they dress the way they do? The people that come here for leisure time and to get away from the hustle and bustle of everyday living, these tourists over forty, why do they dress so goofy... brand new white runners from a well-known budget store, with brand new white socks, I am sure the wife got for him. You know the kind, twelve in a pack, two stripes black, red or blue not ankle or knee length the ones that are in between, those tube socks, one is always lower than the other.

Cotton Bermuda cargo shorts with big pockets on each thigh. Some kind of bright floral shirt usually hibiscus flower pattern and a big honkin' camera hanging around their neck, always getting in the way! A straw hat that they have bartered for, that says Corona or something relating to Puerto Vallarta, sits on their head. It has been out in the rain and is flopping down in front or to the side. Then to top it off if they have been here a few days, they are beet red with sunburn in the face and back and of course their knees. The younger set wouldn't think of dressing that way. They are in the latest gear and top of the line name brand products, their hats are coveted by all the beach venders and timeshare hawkers. They look awesome!

We were having a great time, Gab was getting tips left and right and the tourists were happy. Renato's place caters to a lot of English speaking people so it was quite easy to host. I would give the customers ideas on how to make their holiday easier by using cab tricks like confirming the cost before you get in and shut the door, how to barter and how to look for the real silver mark on jewellery. I told the customers how much the waiters make working here in Mexico and how their tips are their main source of income. When it was busy I didn't get to talk personally with them but in general I got to help them in some way. They were always full of questions. Some really dumb questions that if you thought for one moment they could answer themselves; others, very important questions that they probably should have asked their travel agent before leaving home. It's so funny when people are on holidays and when you come from the same country but lived four thousand miles away from them, they think and act like you were neighbours …ha-ha… yeah we are Canadian best friends and we all live in igloos!

Christmas Eve was a wonderful night, so busy we could hardly keep up. There was a young couple on their honeymoon. He was a king crab fisherman from Alaska and they had come into the restaurant a little early, so I got to talk to them for a while about their story. It was so nice. At the end of the evening we went to "tip out" and there wasn't one peso in the tip jar! Do you believe that, well it was true! They had all paid by credit card… Now, when people pay using "plastic" the restaurant doesn't get the money right away, it goes to the country of the credit card company first and to their bank then back to the Mexican bank here then to the restaurant's bank so it's about seven to ten working days before the workers get their tips. The bigger restaurants don't quite have the same procedures but that was ours. I was devastated not for me and my son because we were fine, but for the cooks, the waiters and the other bartender it was awful. Then I found out that it all comes back to the owner in one lump sum and it takes such a long time for the funds to get back that the owners don't remember how much to pay the workers for their tips! The workers don't remember how much was owed to them and they don't have any proof of what was owed for what day, so they don't get anything. From then on I told the people to pay the tip in cash and put the rest on their credit card if they chose to. I couldn't believe what was going on! From that day until New Year's Day the tip jars were full of cash.

Christmas day I was walking along the Malecón going to meet a friend for brunch and I ran into the young newlywed man from Alaska that was at the restaurant the night before. He said he was on his own that day; that his bride wasn't in very good shape from the evening before. He said he left her hugging the porcelain bowl in their hotel room. He asked if we made a lot in tips the night before. I told him what had happened and he reached into his pocket and pulled out a handful of crumpled pesos and handed them to me saying, "Here, take this for you and your son."

I said, "Oh, no! I didn't tell you that to get any money from you."

He laughed and said, "Please, take this there's lots more where this came from. Please! I don't know how much is there but I don't care. I have lots of that funny money! Merry Christmas! By the way, the lobster was unbelievable! I fish for a living and I know Alaska King Crab and lobster. Thanks again for the great night and the tourist tips you gave us."

He had given me over one hundred dollars' worth of pesos. That was a great tip indeed. He told me he would be going back to the restaurant again for another fabulous meal before they left and he would make sure all the staff received the tips that he felt they had earned. He was a very nice young man.

I wished him well, and told him where to take his bride if she wasn't feeling better within a day.

I was so shocked with the ethics of the restaurant industry here in Mexico and disappointed in my friend's attitude toward his workers that I never worked for him again. I thanked my angels for their guidance in making me so aware of the way things are run in this city. Having insight gave me a lot of power when it came to making any future decisions.

DRUGS AND THE YOUNG MEXICAN GIRL

When we transcend our suffering we rise with the angels.

In Puerto Vallarta I got to meet a lot of people, locals and visitors alike and I have to admit that living there and loving the people I forgot that I am white and not one of them. But inside I never felt the separation; I always felt I was one of the locals. Sometimes I would be reminded by a comment, "Who do you think you are, Mexican?" or "For God's sake, you are a woman, white and Canadian. You should step back and get back into reality."

Sometimes, being white, sometimes being Canadian and not Mexican was in my favour. Many a time I used it to get what I wanted. Believe me, many a time I took advantage of this!

I met a very lovely young Mexican girl in her early twenties. She was tall and slender with beautiful long black silky hair like in a TV hair advertisement. She was from Cancun. Let's just call her Marlene. She was here to get a job. Her father was some well-to-do man and she wanted to be out on her own and independent. Well, she did that all right. I used to see her every few days and ask her how things were going. She was a friend of a friend of mine and that's how I met her. She would drop by the house every now and then or I would see her in the street. She would update me on her life.

I was to meet her one night for drinks and she didn't show up. A few days went by and still no word. So I asked her friend where the little stinker had been hiding and he said she was in jail. He said that she had been at a bar with her boyfriend and the police came in and checked everyone's purse and they arrested her. She had been carrying drugs that her boyfriend had put in her purse and when they searched her, they just took her away. She had made it clear that the drugs weren't hers and she didn't even know they were in her purse, but that didn't seem to matter to the *policía*. The boyfriend had disappeared of course! So she was taken to the local police station, questioned and then transferred, and was in jail in Guadalajara awaiting trial. Apparently, according to gossip, she was about to be sentenced to one year in jail.

A month later there was a knock on my door and I open the door and there she was looking like hell, her hair a mess, dirty, oily, and matted and probably not combed or washed for the entire time she was gone. She was so run down. She looked like what we would call the wrath of God. Her clothes were filthy stained and in tatters. She just collapsed in my arms and I held her for a moment and carried her in my arms to the sofa where she started to sob. She cried and cried.

We finally looked at each other; she took a deep breath and started to talk. This is where I want to make it clear that this is the story that she told me and I have no way of verifying it so I will tell it as it was told to me.

The guards raped her repeatedly the entire time she was there. They deprived her of sleep and emotionally, physically and sexually abused her. The stories she told me, about what they made her do, I could hardly listen to! She was fed almost nothing and she had no family to bring her food so she never had three square meals a day or a proper bed to sleep on. She was not allowed to bath or keep herself clean like we would feel entitled to in a Canadian jail.

Her experience in jail was just horrendous. I couldn't believe the story I was hearing. I was in tears just listening. I couldn't believe what she was telling me and all I could do was shake my head. This lovely girl had these traumatic and horrible memories of the events that she experienced and I feel will probably never completely recover from.

I asked her how she stayed sane during that time. She looked at me with her beautiful soft brown eyes and said, "I pretended it wasn't me and went into a different world."

She said she was released because she told them who her father was and they recognized his name. They knew that he had money so they said if he sent them 80,000 pesos they would let her go. To get the money to the right people for this to happen however took time and in the meantime she continued to be abused.

I gave her some soup and a cup of tea and showed her where the bathroom was and gave her everything she needed to have a hot shower and clean herself up. She came out of the bathroom with a smile on her face wearing a towel on her head and said she couldn't believe how wonderful it felt to use soap, shampoo and conditioner and to finally be able to brush her teeth. She laughed and said, "I think I brushed my teeth ten times."

Fortunately, I had some clothes that fit her and gave her an outfit of clean things to wear that she could keep. I gave her a pair of sandals, a purse and a bundle of cosmetics like lipstick, hand cream, eye shadow and hair clips and I then threw her old clothes into the trash.

I asked her how she was able to get to my house and she said she hitchhiked from Guadalajara (about five hours if you go by bus) and she prayed that I would be home when she arrived. Her family had been contacted and the jailors told her that they had been given 80,000 pesos and she was released but she would need to find her own way home.

She contacted her family and after she stayed with me for a few days they wired her money to travel from my place to her family's home. I took her to the bus depot, wished her well, kissed her and told her that it would be a good idea when she got home to get some counseling about the ordeal that she had been through. I said just ignoring it would not make it go away.

I was fortunate enough to have previously received as a gift from a Canadian First Nations princess some leather beaded hat band strips. When they were gifted to me I was instructed to cut one off and pass it on by tying it onto the wrist of anyone I felt was in trouble and needed spiritual help from Father Sky and Mother Earth. I cut a strip and tied it to her wrist. She was visibly moved by my gesture and the hope of spiritual protection.

I told her I felt she should report what had happened in the jail and that they should be held accountable for their actions and she was startled. She made it very clear that she was afraid to do anything about it. She said she could never even tell anyone about what happened because they would never believe her, nor could she ever prove it to be true.

... So there you go. It doesn't matter who you are "shit happens." It happens if you're Mexican, Canadian or no matter where you live or what your station in life.

I never did see or hear from her again and I hope to this day she is doing well. I wish you well, Marlene.

The angels that helped you get out of jail and get home will always be with you.

MEETING SAMMIE AND MANDI

Often we find the person we least expected it from, sprouts wings and becomes our angel.

I was working at the most horrible job I have ever encountered, which by the way was on my shortlist of deleting from my life. I was in timeshare sales. I was awful at it...I could be a 'liner', which is someone who tours you around the hotel and tells you why you should invest in this operation. I could do that, but a 'closer'- no, no. When people said no to me, I couldn't get passed that wall.

I was on my way home, and was about two blocks from my place where I usually stopped to talk to the owner of a small bar where you could play pool, crib and backgammon, drink a beer and listen to some music. The owner would greet me with, "How is the most beautiful woman in Puerto Vallarta?"

I would reply, "How's the most handsome man in Vallarta?" I dropped in to see Mortie and he wasn't in but the girl behind the bar told me he wouldn't be long and he mentioned earlier that he wanted to see me, so I stayed. I was in the middle of drinking a cold Corona when a woman walked in looking exhausted, dragging a very large suitcase behind her. She sat down and ordered a Double XX. I noticed that she had Canadian cigarettes so I said, "Are you from Canada and where?" She told me her name and proceeded to tell me where she was from and to let me know why she was in the bar. She seemed to need to share what had happened to her and her boyfriend. He was still out wandering around trying to find a place to stay. She bought me a drink and continued her story. By the time she was finished, her boyfriend Sammie walked in, shaking his head and said, "There is nothing around here. Everything is booked for the weekend. Some kind of Mexican holiday!"

I liked them from the beginning. They both were from a small town up north in British Columbia where my sister lived for years. They had a few more drinks and we chatted about this and that and then I suggested that they stay with me for the night; that I had an extra room and then they could continue looking for a place the next day. They agreed and were quite relieved. They said they would take me out for dinner and I thought that was great. I told them I only lived a couple of blocks away and that was a relief as well. I looked up and noticed Mortie come in and he joined us.

We walked home talking about the reason they had come down and when we entered my place they commented on how nice it was. I showed them their room and they took their gear in and came out of the bedroom asking me if they could stay at my place for the week and they would pay me for the room. I said, "Sure! That sounds like a win-win situation for all of us."

The next day, they had to meet with a realtor to look at some condos they had seen online. Later in the day they returned not too happy, seeing the places personally was not the same as looking at the pictures, so they made some more appointments for other places. Sammie wanted to buy in the one week they were there. He had his mind set on what he wanted and that was that. He also mentioned that his driver was on his way down with the mayor of his hometown and they had to pick them up at the airport and find them a place to stay. I looked at him and shook my head and said, "No, no, *no!* What do you think I am? I do not run a bed and breakfast house."

He laughed and said, "Just wait and if you like them you tell me okay? They are only here for three days."

The following day, they went to the airport and within a few hours I had two more guests. *My goodness! What is this all about?* I wondered. They were no trouble and they went out searching for the perfect place, which they found. It was in a brand new high rise in Mismaloya. By the fifth day it was a done deal. They would be back in a month and asked if they could come to my place till they got settled and I once more agreed.

Sammie was the manager of a racing team and wasn't planning on doing that anymore. He had done it for years and he had had enough. His dream was to live in a hot country and operate a sports bar. He still had to finish that year's racing circuit but after that, he was in Vallarta for the long haul. The following month they returned and I had quit timeshare and was doing nothing. We sat on the balcony talking over his long term plans. He was aware that I had owned a restaurant in B.C. and we talked about that. He wanted me to be a part of his dream and I wasn't sure if I wanted that or not. I told him I would think about it. He was going again but Mandi was staying and we would talk about it upon his return in the next two months. When he returned we talked and talked. He wanted to look for a venue and wanted me to supervise the construction of his dream. I was very aware that it was his dream not mine and he was the head honcho and Mandi and I really didn't have too much to say about it. He would listen to our ideas and our input but in the end, it was all going to be up to him...his money his dream...

I was blessed with the opportunity to go through the process of creating and physically building a new bar. I had always wanted to experience the challenge of dealing with the "red tape" and political hoops that were placed before me. It was a growth opportunity in itself.

MY PURSE STOLEN RIGHT UNDER MY NOSE

The white noise of worry will block out the angelic words.

Some days can be going very nicely and everything falling into place and the world is looking wonderful and you are so glad to be alive, then *whammo!*

It happened on a Tuesday in June. I had just received my money from my ex-husband and had gone to pay my rent and came home with a few articles from the drugstore that I needed. I walked through my front door and placed my purse on the counter and went to the bathroom. There was a knock on my door and it was the Mexican gentleman from up one flight up, his suite was directly above me. In his broken English he asked if he could take a look at his cable line that was attached to the telephone pole located just off my balcony. I said, "Sure." I didn't realize at the time he had been cut off his cable due to non-payment. He went out to the box, which was just a hand reach away, and did something. I wasn't too interested. He came back in and thanked me and proceeded to the front door. He was facing me, and then he turned and leaned against the corner of the counter, then turned and walked out the door. I shut the door and went into the kitchen.

I put away the articles from the drugstore and went to get my purse to hide the rest of my money and I couldn't see my purse. I thought, *Oh, you silly girl you took it to the bathroom when you came in.* I went to the bathroom and no purse. Well, I knew I had my purse when I came home because my keys were on the chain on the zipper and I couldn't get in without it, because my door locks automatically when it shuts. It was a pain in the ass because you couldn't do anything without having my key on me. I was in a panic. I knew by now that asshole upstairs had taken it. While I was looking in my fridge I was thinking, *Who knows where it is?* I was in panic mode!

At that moment, I heard a friend yell out my name from outside. I called him in and told Nacho the story. He went up to the neighbours and I could hear him screaming in Spanish at my neighbour. He came downstairs and said, "Let's go to the police." Before we left we took a knife, placed it in the door jamb so that we could get back in. The police station was only a block away so we were there in seconds.

Nacho interpreted everything for me. I was crying and crying. I could hardly speak.

They took my statement in triplicate, which took two hours and by the way, it is done with a police officer and a typist typing by hand with carbon paper on a manual typewriter and three plain pieces of paper, they had maybe fifteen copies by the time we finished. Then they went to the neighbour and nothing happened! He said he didn't touch anything and that was that. I was hysterical because my purse contained my two Visas, my debit card, my house keys, every cent I had, my Mexican bank card, my driver's license and birth certificate...every business card necessary to function in Puerto Vallarta, and my phone book, all that was important to me. Fortunately, my passport and plane ticket home were kept in a different spot. After a couple of hours at the police station we returned to my suite.

I was a mess. Nina, a girl friend of mine was, as previously arranged, was on her way over to meet me to go to the beach. When she arrived, Nacho told her the story, because I was still crying. She said, "Let's go for a drink at Martie's bar."

I said, "*Right!* How can I do that? I don't have one cent and no key to unlock my door!"

Nina said, "Never mind, shut the door and we will climb in the balcony when we return."

She suggested, "Leave the balcony door shut but not locked and we will get my husband to climb the tree and jump to your balcony and open the door to let us in."

I didn't want to go but there was no reason to stay home and cry. Nothing could be done and I didn't know what to do. It didn't matter that I had money in the bank at home I didn't have any way to get the money out. I was screwed! I couldn't even phone my ex-husband because I didn't even have five pesos to get the operator to phone collect to talk to anyone...so off we go to the bar.

While we were walking to the bar we saw the neighbour's wife getting out of their car with a bunch of groceries. Nacho yelled something at her in Spanish and she just put her head down and ran into the apartment. "*Oh! You did it all right!*" he screamed at her. Nacho gave another comment to me, "I will fix them. I will put sugar in their gas tank later on!"

I just looked at him in disapproval but to be very honest I thought of a lot worse things to do to them! So off we went to the bar.

At the bar we were telling everyone and anyone who would listen, our story and of course they couldn't believe it. So as we are having a beer and the owner of the bar was hugging me and telling me it's going to be okay and we will all work something out, Nina is telling a stranger from the United States what had happened. He came over to me and asked me how I was doing and introduced himself as Raye something. I wasn't really paying much attention to him. I really didn't want to meet someone new. Nacho had to leave and go to work and he said he would be passing by tomorrow with some money for me. I gave him a hug and he prepared to leave.

In the meantime, Raye asked, "How are you going to get back into your home?"

I say, "I don't know. I don't even have eighty pesos to get a locksmith to come and change the lock and give me a new set of keys."

He said, "Well, you do now. Where is the locksmith?"

That was all it took and I was bawling my head off again. Nacho hadn't left and said he would go to the locksmith on the way to work. He went to the locksmith next door to the bar and told him our problem. The locksmith said he could come in two or three hours and do it but he was busy right then. We said fine come and get us at the bar when you're ready and we will go to my place with you. We stayed there going over and over what had happened until he came. We walked the two blocks home with the locksmith and I got new keys and a new lock before the night was over.

Raye asked, "Now what are you going to do?"

I just looked at him and my eyes filled with tears again. I was in such a state I couldn't think or even answer him. He looked at me. "Well, then, I guess I will do the thinking." He suggested I go and find my Visa numbers, phone numbers, codes and serial numbers and account information so I did and as I was looking for them my glasses fell off my face and hit the marble floor and they broke. Believe *that!* I looked at the floor and my glasses and I looked at Raye, he looked at the glasses and then back at me. I sat on my bed and put my face in my hands and just shook my head. He just hugged me and laughed and said, "Okay, I guess I have to see for you too. Now go have a bath or shower, freshen up and get dressed and we will go out for dinner, but in the meantime just try to relax. Let's have a coffee and go somewhere nice to have dinner."

I said, "Why are you doing this? You don't even know me; you just met me hours ago. *Why?*"

He just looked at me and said, "Why not?"

The two of us, Nina and her husband, who had met us at the bar after work, went to dinner, then dancing and he brought me home in his car. Raye started to tell me a little about himself. He had driven down from California after visiting his daughter. He was a widower, his wife died a few years back from cancer and he had nothing better to do so he thought he would drive down to Puerto Vallarta and visit with some buddies who lived there. At the end of the evening he told me to go to bed and get some rest; he would be here at nine the next morning and take me to breakfast and do some things.

I said, "What things?"

"You'll see," he whispered.

I looked at him and nodded, went to bed and cried myself to sleep. The next morning, sure enough there he was knocking on my door. "Good morning, sunshine, let's go, it's a beautiful day," he said. So we go to breakfast and talk for hours and then afterwards we got my glasses fixed and went out for a lovely lunch.

While we were waiting to get my glasses repaired with new lenses, he got me some new frames and insisted that I get a pair of contacts just because he wanted to look at my beautiful blue eyes without any glasses over them. He said I was the most beautiful woman he had seen or met in years...I stated that he must need new glasses. Raye said, "So what if you think I am blind? I like what I see!" We made arrangements to have new glasses and to come back in three days for the contacts and we went home. He was very soft-spoken and very easy going and I liked his demeanor. He was quiet, but so together and an inner strength that made me calm.

I went to lie down for a while and he left to visit his buddies at the hotel. I didn't ask where. He told me he would be back and take me out to dinner and wanted me to meet a friend that played the piano in the lounge at the hotel where we could have a nice evening. I agreed and asked him to pick me up around eight. At this point I am wondering, *Is this another angel in my life?*

We walked to his car and he said, "I don't like driving in Puerto Vallarta. Will you do the driving?" From then on I drove us everywhere. I just didn't know what to think of this wonderful man and what he was doing for me. It was now three days since we met and he asked, "Have you done anything about your Visa?"

I looked at him and answered, "How am I going to do that? I don't have the funds to do anything and I truly don't know where to start."

"You are coming with me to a hotel," he said. "It is by the water with a beautiful beachfront and this is our room for a few days?

I exclaimed, "What? *No way!* I live just down the street. Why would I come and stay on the beach like this?"

He sighed, "Because you need to get away from there and concentrate on doing your business by phoning Canada and letting Visa, MasterCard, your ex and everyone know what has happened. Do the things you have to do to get things right. Now write a list of what you have to do and I'll be back in half an hour. Now *do it!*"

He came back with a bottle of Coke and a few chocolate bars some chips and peanuts, now he smiled, "Eat this junk you like and make those phone calls. I told the desk to charge the phone calls to me. I'll now see you in an hour, so get busy!"

I stopped him and thanked him but made it quite clear that I was not going to sleep with him just because he was doing this. If that was the real reason for the kind and wonderful act it could stop now and I would go home. He just looked at me and said, "I'd love to sleep with you beautiful lady but I don't think you have to worry. I don't think I could get it up anyway. It's been too many years."

I just laughed and said I would make the calls.

A few hours later it was all done. Raye then made me phone my ex to ask him to send down by FedEx a debit card that I had at home because the bank wouldn't issue a new one without me coming into the bank to get it. He sent me his old one that was on my bank account and recorded it with my password so I could get some money. It would take a few working days for it to arrive. It was now Friday so I had to wait till at least the following Wednesday to get it. Raye was pleased that now everything was in order, Visa was sending new cards and cancelled the old one. "You can get a new driver's license when you go home. Whenever that will be, which should be in the near future," he reassured me.

"Now where are we going?" I muttered.

He winked at me and said, "We are going shopping!"

I stared at him in bewilderment. He stated with a very strong voice, "For toothpaste, toilet paper, groceries ...You have nothing in the house. You didn't have the money on you, it was in your purse right? You still need those things, don't you?"

"Okay, okay," I said.

We had a wonderful twenty-seven days after the chaos. Then he told me he had to go home for cancer treatments and would phone me in Canada because he would be back in the fall. It was the hardest goodbye I had ever experienced – sometimes having to say goodbye really hurts.

He phoned Carmen in Canada and told her I was doing fine and he was going to get a newer car because he thought I would like that. He was driving back to Puerto Vallarta to surprise me and we could drive to Canada if I wanted. I know this because she phoned me in Mexico and told me of the strange phone call from someone named Raye who said after his treatments in California he was coming back. This wonderful man never came back and I never heard from him again. I have the feeling the treatments didn't go well. I think of him often and wish I could contact him but maybe the only way is through my prayers. Amen.

God sent me an angel when I needed it the most. This was one of the worst times in my life. When you are four thousand miles away from home and can't do anything, it's scary and the feeling of the loss of control and helplessness couldn't be expressed in words, but those who have been there know! When things like this experience happen out of the blue I must believe in a power greater than myself taking care of me. Don't you think?

To me, angels exist but sometimes, just sometimes, when we don't think they are with us, they are... but maybe in the form of a friend.

DICKS...TO THE LEFT

In all our comings and goings, at the end of the day when we place our head on our pillow we must remember to thank the angels for their guidance.

This adventure took place in a good old bar that I happen to enjoy very much. I love the people who congregate at this watering hole. This place had craggy used brick walls with arches at the entrance. There were more arches inside that open up into the different areas where one could sit and relax. The area I liked to sit in was semi private. I could bring friends in and lounge and talk or socialize. From this spot we enjoyed watching the new customers that wandered in and out. They would be walking up the sidewalk and before they had reached the bar they could see in the distance a blue hue reflecting out onto the street from the windows and through the large arched entrance. Some were very curious and would peep in and others wandered in and looked around and left.

Many tourists came in and stayed for a drink or two while lounging on a puffy upholstered long L-shaped sofa in a private corner or on the high bar stools covered with a fabric that was an abstract pattern of black and white. The tables were set up for couples wanting a glass of wine or for a group that just wanted to have Tequila shots and carry on. Some customers chose to stand while others sat at the long marble bar looking up. One could gaze at the displayed bottles of many kinds of spirits that looked like they were all at attention to say, "*Pick me! Pick me!*"

After you had chosen your "poison", you found yourself looking into the mirrored wall draped with blue twinkle lights mystically sparkling behind the bartender. The mirror was a great idea because it gave you the opportunity without being too obvious to scan the rooms behind you. Most of the customers at the bar were very entertained by the antics of the bartender making a martini with fresh fruit or with herbs that had been picked that day from the owner's garden.

My girlfriend and I were having a drink in our new home away from home called the Rockwall. It was made very clear to me a few months prior when we started frequently coming to this bar that I was the 'queen' of the establishment. Whatever I wanted I could have for the asking. It did make me a little snobbish, I must admit. We had been there that particular evening for a while and were on our third martini when I had to go to the bathroom, as most due after consuming a large amount of liquids, so I got up and proceeded to go to the ladies room. It was occupied, so I waited patiently for the door to open.

A man walked out, I gave him a look of "What the hell are you doing in my bathroom?" I proceeded to gesture with my arms extended...The men's is to the left! The first *left*! He then passed me and returned to the bar area where I had noticed him earlier. The reason I noticed him was because he was a very good looking black dude, very tall and broad with very sharp features and a gorgeous Colgate smile. Puerto Vallarta doesn't have a lot of black tourists. I have no idea why but they don't visit here. In twenty years, I bet I can count on one hand how many I have seen. One that I met became a friend years ago and still lives in Vallarta.

I had entered the bathroom and then shut the door, when I looked down and I could see that he had urinated all over the seat and on the floor! I was furious. I opened the door and marched right up to him and said with a very stern voice, "Young man, come with me!" He had a look of confusion, he looked around and we walked to the bathroom and I pointed out to him saying, "How could you leave this bathroom in this state? There is urine all over the place! This, by the way, is not your bathroom, it is for ladies!"

He just stared at me and said, "What the hell! There is no sign that says that! Why didn't you use the other one?"

I just looked at him. I shouted, "The other one only has a urinal!"

"*Too bad!*"he roared and under his breath, just loud enough for me to hear, "*Bitch!*" and started to turn and walk away.

I turned him around and slapped him on the face while in a tone of speech that seemed to stop him in his tracks I continued to bellow, "You *pig!*"and I slammed the door in his face and proceeded to clean up his mess with the supplies in the corner of the room. I shouldn't have done it, but I really needed to use the toilet.

In the meantime, apparently, he walked up to the bar counter and demanded to talk to the owner and proceeded to tell him in a very loud voice that I had slapped him on the face! Marcus replied, "Well, if she did that to you there must have been a good reason, that's not her style." The guy asked for his bill and left.

When I came out of the ladies' room, I walked into a crowd of men that were staring at me from the bar. The owner Marcus was walking towards me laughing and shaking his head from left to right as if saying...what have you done now? As he put his arm around me and took me to my seat on the sofa in the corner of the room, he asked me what had happened. I told him that I had just got rid of a new customer! He probably wouldn't be back!

I disclosed to him the story with others eavesdropping. I finished explaining the event and they all laughed and turned back to their drinks. One of the customers said very loudly to everyone, "Oh my god...don't mess with her my friends, if you have a dick you better go to the left!"

Marcus said hysterically, "*No!* The *first* left!"

I sat down with Lynda. Her mouth was wide open and looking a little stunned, shaking her head, I told her what had happened in greater detail and she just stared at me, "Are you nuts? He could have hit you back and really hurt you for God's sake...That guy was over six feet tall!"

I just shook my head and said, "I guess you're right but I was so angry and felt so violated when he refused to clean it up or take any responsibility for his actions I just reacted." Well, maybe I wouldn't have done it quite that way if I hadn't had three martinis but to be very honest if I hadn't been drinking, I probably would have punched him.

This predicament relates to me having to stand up for myself, which by the way I do not do well. It seems to have to be a life-threatening situation before I do something about it... I have a tendency to be the peacemaker and the one that cleans up the problems, fixes it or makes everything harmonious, even to my detriment. Eventually, the need to stand up for myself builds up and it only awaits a triggering incident and then *kaboom*, the over reaction is out of my control.

As for the angels in this story? I think they were looking after me. Of that I am quite sure!

WANDA AND THE PARASAILOR

We are all hugged by angels but some of us never open our arms.

One evening I was alone walking in my neighbourhood looking at the changes taking place and the beautiful colourful flowers hanging from the very large tropical plants with the wind moving the branches and the trees waving in the wind. Almost every corner and sidewalk, every street at this time of year was breathtaking. The evening was a warm one and I was enjoying my stroll, when a mood to just talk to the locals came over me.

I decided to go into a nearby cantina where the tourists did not hang out. It was nice to talk to the regulars and just socialize without any work topics. While I was there I decided to tell a joke. The joke went this way...What does a Mexican girl, an American girl and Canadian girl say after having sex? The Mexican girl says, "I have never done this before;" the American says "What's your name again?" and the Canadian girl says, "That's it?"... There was a pause and nothing...I seemed to be the only one that thought it was funny, and then I heard someone hysterically laughing in the corner of the room. I turned towards the laughter and saw a little blonde woman and I put up my arm and said very loudly, "You must be Canadian!" She nodded yes... I gestured to her to come to my table and I would buy her a drink.

I found out that she was in Puerto Vallarta for the long haul. Wanda worked as a bartender in the marina; she had been there for eight months so far and was doing quite well. She said that she hung out with the parasailors which intrigued me. I didn't know any parasailors personally but I had heard a lot about them. They were a special breed of their own. Their style of dress was unique, their hairstyle was a little different from the rest of the young men in the tourist industry. They were out on the beach from morning till night, they could swim like fish and when they were in the water they seemed to become a part of the wave. For whatever reason, which I never did find out, they never came into town after dark or came into the clubs. Wanda said they have their own community and that's where they stay after work. Every time I was with Wanda and she had her boyfriend with her, she had to vouch for him and fight to get him into the bar or club.

Wanda was unique in her own way; she was a tough little cookie having had a very hard upbringing. She said, "I wasn't brought up I was dragged up." I was part of some of her experiences in Puerto Vallarta. One night, I ran into her at a disco and she was very, very intoxicated and I was walking in to meet her as the police were taking her out yelling and screaming at the top of her lungs. Wanda had left her purse in the bar after the police had removed her from the place. The police said I could get her in the morning, that she would be there all night. The next day I went to the police station to get Wanda but she wasn't there. I asked one of the officers I knew what had happened. He just shook his head and said, "We let her go last night, it took four of us to get her in the cell and when we did get her in the cell and shut the door she grabbed the bars and kicked and wiggled and moved so violently we gave up and told her to get the hell out of the precinct. So she did, swearing and cursing in Spanish and English."

I thanked him for the information and left to go to her home. I arrived at her home and after knocking and knocking on her door she finally answered, looking like hell, covered in bruises.

We started to talk, with her telling me the whole night's story and how come she was arrested. At one point I asked if she was ever afraid. She said, "Hell no! Are you kidding? I wasn't staying there no matter what!"

I also asked how she got into her apartment. Wanda informed me that she climbed up the balconies to her floor and went through the balcony doors that were unlocked. I just looked at her... "Are you kidding me? You live on the *sixth floor*! You could have killed yourself. My god, Wanda!"

"Yeah I know but I didn't, I had no choice. I need to get changed. My clothes were all ripped and I needed to have a bath."

I stayed friends with her for about two years and one day after not seeing her for a while I checked with the parasailing boyfriend and he said he hadn't seen her for a couple of weeks. I went out to the bar where she worked and they said she just didn't come in for her shift and they hadn't seen her since. I never did hear from her again I sure hope she went back home and all is well.

PEYOTE – THE NO NO DRINK

Angels are never against us; they are always on our side.

Being in Puerto Vallarta for about five months, Gab had a friend of his come down for a visit. We decided to take him to the restaurant where Gab worked as a bartender and I worked as a hostess every now and then when they were short-staffed. I will start this story by letting you know how I met Pancho, the owner of the restaurant and how I got to know a lot of young men in Puerto Vallarta.

I went to Puerto Vallarta with my daughter for a week's vacation and we were told to go to a place called Chukka's Place to eat a nice dinner and stay and dance for the evening. The first night we arrived at this little fishing village we went to this establishment. Carmen, my daughter, is very beautiful long blonde hair, nice body, of course she was twenty, and lovely perfect smile. Well, to me, she is stunning. But of course all daughters are beautiful to their mothers.

We arrived and the guys were all over her like bees to honey and we were being fought over on who was to serve us. Truly, it was something to watch at that time in my life. I was still married and I had lost quite a few pounds, starting off at 330 pounds and now I was down to about 186 pounds so I was still big and didn't want to dance, so she did and I stood with a coffee on the balcony and watched the men fight over her. I was very proud. They knew nothing was going to get past me as I watched. Anyway in the week we were there she made some female friends that lived there and they took her many places and so did the young men.

I had a restaurant in Canada and the young man standing beside me watching Carmen on the dance floor one evening introduced himself to me and gave me his card, which was for his restaurant. He invited us up there for dinner on him, so we went the next night and a relationship started from there. They came to visit in Canada and we had a great time. So when I decided to move there I was already established with some new friends and when Gab needed a job, Pancho gave him a job. The two young men Rico and Jose, were friends by now and had visited us in Canada and I found out in the process that many of my friends knew Pancho already so when they visited me we would go there for dinner and out dancing so Pancho got to know a lot of my friends as well.

Now, back to the peyote...we went with Gab and his buddy to the restaurant. There were four of us: his friend Dino, Dianna, Gab and myself. We had dinner and a couple of tequila shooters and then out came the rheas, which is tequila but made from the roots of the plant and is very, very strong. It's against the law but everyone has some tucked away under the table. It's like white lightning – one tablespoon will put you under the table. And when you have some everyone knows it because it smells like sour milk, like baby vomit... So, they all have a shot and wouldn't let me. Then out came the peyote – this is the roots and seeds of the tequila plant, which are fermented. This is what the shamans drink to hallucinate and go into a trance ...not good to fool around with.

Everyone took a shot but me. There were many glasses on the table: tequila shots, recia, and peyote and I grab a tequila shot and as I'm downing it with lime my son shouts at me, "*No, Mom, no! That's peyote!* Too late – it's down. Dinner was over and we were off to do some dancing. By the way, my son doesn't dance; don't know why, he just doesn't. He does a lot of socializing and talking at the bar, but that's it. So off we went down this very long steep hill to the Malecón. We got to the main street and I went left and met a friend and I stared to talk. I looked around and no Gab, Dianna or Dino. I couldn't find Gab so I went to the Cage and I knew he was around somewhere. I got into the Cage, it was crowded but you know me, I just passed everyone and got in and start to talk to more friends as I worked my way to the back to the bathroom. That took about one hour because by the time I hit the bathroom it was eleven o'clock, which I noticed, for some strange reason.

I went into one of the stalls and sat down. I put my head on the side of the wall and sat there a few minutes. Well, I thought it was a few minutes. I looked at my watch and it was 1:00 a.m. in the morning I had been sitting there for two hours and it went so fast. No one came to check on me, there was a bathroom attendant in there at all times and I don't think she checked. Can you believe that? As I start to get up I realized I couldn't move my legs. I tried to pick them up and nothing happened so I sat there. I didn't say a word as I waited. What I was waiting for I don't really know. I then looked at my watch again and it was now around 2:00 a.m. and I still couldn't move. A few minutes later I think, *I can get up*, and then I was standing. I straightened my clothes and put on my cowboy hat and I visualized in my head how to get out of the place: out of the bathroom, down the aisle to the main bar, down three steps, turn right, down five stairs to the door, into a taxi and I'm home.

I started and when I got to the opening where you slightly turn to go down the five stairs, I walked straight into the wall. I didn't turn. I heard Sergio at the door say, "What the hell is wrong with you, Sheila?" and the next thing I knew I was at my door. The taxi guy Tony, thank God, had taken me to my door and helped me get in. The next thing I knew it was morning and I was awake and wondering how I got there …This has only happened once before in my life but that's another story! I walked into the front room and Gab was nursing his head and just looked at me, eyes bloodshot and said nothing, pointed to the other sofa and there was his friend, face down. Gab told me he ended up at Crystals, another big fancy nightclub and he was dancing in the middle of the floor with his shirt off with Dianna dancing along with him. He said he lost Dino, didn't know where he went and found himself at our door around five in the morning saying he found himself on some bridge vomiting his guts out and then he was under the bridge and crawled up the bank and got a cab and came home. Not remembering much of anything!

The last night Dino was in town we went to the Cage and Gabriel said to me, "You came down those stairs the other night looking like a ghost and your eyes were glassy and you didn't say a word and walked right into the wall. Tony was outside and he took you home!

"I have never seen you like that before ever!! We knew something was terribly wrong! What happened to you? What the hell happened? Everyone was so worried about you!"

I told him the story and all he could do was laugh and shake his head because he knew that I would never do that on purpose. *What a night!*

CANADIAN/MEXICAN WEDDING

*When two become one a new life starts with
the angels guiding their open hearts.*

This story is a "Love Story."
I'd like to start by telling you about my friends Deedee and Fernando with whom I am still friends and in touch with today.

Deedee is a very pretty young woman with short sandy blonde hair and blue eyes, a little on the plump side, which it seems is how a lot of Mexican men like their women. She is Canadian who had always been single and Fernando is Mexican, I think. I never did find out exactly. He said he was from Puerto Rico from a very large family. The truth about his nationality I don't know. His face features and colouring weren't *"Mexican."* He was previously married and had two kids that he didn't see and I never asked why.

I don't know to this day their last names; never knew Deedee's maiden name and I can't remember Fernando's. If I had to find out, it wouldn't be a problem getting it. I got into the habit of not caring about people's names or what they used to do before they came to PV. It's what they are in my life that matters. Sometimes not knowing is a good thing.

Fernando was a waiter I met two years prior to meeting Deedee. I met him on his first day of work at a bar called Coco's located on the Malecón. This place catered to people who loved to do line dancing in their windows. When certain songs played everyone would climb up onto the window ledges and dance a routine. Then, when the song was over the bartenders, the shooter girls and waiters would go back to what they were doing and the place carried on.

Fernando waited on me, and I liked him right off the top. We started to talk and our friendship grew from there. Fernando had light brown long hair and hazel eyes. His skin was a fairly light olive colour and he had a Roman nose (like the statue of David) and an awesome smile with very pearly whites. Very easy to look at, and his ability to speak English helped a lot. With him working there every night we became very close. He let me know that if I had more meat on my bones I would be perfect...I laughed out loud and from that point on we were friends. Not that anything else was ever going to be, but it was nice to know that I was more than just another customer.

After a while Fernando got better at his job and he was able to get a position as manager at a different club called Foxy's.

Deedee was in Puerto Vallarta with two of her friends for six months and we all ended up living in the same neighborhood. They were all from Calgary and I got to know them all very well... one was also named Sheila and she was also a Taurus, like me. She was a hairdresser and she would do my hair almost every day and it was wonderful because she was very good at it. Hair is very important to me so her doing a new style for me all the time was just fabulous. The other girl was Michelle I think. We went out a lot together! Deedee and I went to Foxy's one night and she took one look at Fernando and was smitten with him ...love at first sight. They became an *item*. He was younger than her but that didn't seem to matter. He just adored her and still does!

After a while they became inseparable and then one day out of the blue she got really sick and within a week she was on her way to the hospital for an emergency operation. We didn't know why she was sick or what the results were going to be but it was serious, it had something to do with her stomach and we were all very worried. Nobody at the hospital would explain to us what the hell was happening.

During this experience Fernando realized how much he really loved her and if she were to die he would be lost without her. The hospital was just up the street from my place so everyday he would stop by and keep me in the loop. He would sit for hours every day just looking at her and doing what he could. After the operation, which by the way was successful, she was fine within a few weeks, but Fernando was not. He drove me crazy every day. He was down at the bar and up to the hospital. After she recovered he asked her to marry him. She had never been married before. She was very, very nervous that this gorgeous young man who could have anyone he wanted, in her opinion, really wanted her. In spite of her concerns, she said yes. She decided to sell her house in Calgary and take the big leap and move permanently to Mexico. To this day, he will not take any of her money. He believes that the man is the money maker and that's that.

Well, to a Canadian girl that's a little hard to digest but very good in a permanent relationship, believe me, because not all, but a lot of Mexicans are eager to get out of Mexico or to better themselves - whether they are male or female - by being with a foreigner. They use every way they can to get out, including charm, lies and deception. Not Fernando, I believe he really does love her. The Mexican way is to control the wife as much as possible by not allowing them to do much...My god, talk about control and dominance, but that's a story I'll have to write another time. They were getting married and the date was set.

You have to understand the Mexican people and their traditions when it comes to having a wedding and celebrating are not the same as those of a Canadian. First of all, we know that when you send a wedding invitation to a Canadian family, you tell them on the invitation card the details of the marriage and whether or not the invitation includes a partner or escort and those indications are followed exactly by the persons invited. We politely "RSVP" our reply by mail with how many and the names of those who are going to attend. *Well,* in Mexico it doesn't happen that way!

In Mexico, when you send an invitation to a family the whole family comes, literally, that includes mother, father, grandparents, sisters, brothers, and kids it goes on and on! On the wedding day if those invited have guests at their home, they come too! That's how a guest list of 200 ends up with 800 attending. I have personally witnessed this occurrence! This is acceptable and the consequence is people running to the liquor store over and over getting more and more alcohol and women running to the store for more and more food.

This is the *"Mexican Way."*

Deedee's concept of a wedding was *not* the *"Mexican Way!"*

There was quite a dilemma about what they were going to do. What they finally decided was this. They got the invitations and sent them out. The invitation stated that only the people whose names appeared on the card were allowed to attend the wedding. They decided to hire four buses to transport all the guests. When the guests were boarding the buses they were required to hand in their invitation, and only the persons who were named on the card were allowed to board. There were security guards at the bus doors to ensure that if you did not have your invitation, you did not get on board. It was quite an ordeal, but necessary, because when the town of Puerto Vallarta found out that Fernando was getting married, everybody wanted to go! They were inviting themselves, they were going whether they were invited or not. That's just the way it was. Well, Deedee got hold of that rumour and said *"No way!* This is how it's going to be." They decided to have the wedding out of town at a secret location, nobody knew where. You were to get on the bus and they would take you there. *That was that!* The buses would be there to take us back home, running every hour on the hour after the wedding and dinner.

In the meantime, while the invitations were being hand delivered, it was decided to have a colour code for the wedding. They chose a fabric called Manta. It is a cream-coloured cotton gauze material but any cream coloured fabric was also acceptable. No other solid colour. The manta could have a woven pattern on it but only cream colored. Everyone one had to wear it!

A friend of ours had an up and coming business there ...she was an unbelievable designer and dressmaker. She was hired to create the bride's dress and make the groom's and best man's outfits, as well as the bridesmaid's gowns. The whole enchilada!She even made my dress. It was unique and very beautiful and I still wear it on special occasions today especially when I return to my second home in Puerto Vallarta; unless my youngest son is there and tells me not to "wear any of your Mexican shit."

There were hundreds of people going to the wedding. We all assembled early in the morning on the Malecón, which is a general meeting area in PV where many people connect. The Elite Buses were all lined up waiting for us. I saw the four buses all in a row as I arrived. The security guards were in uniform standing by the doors waiting. The people were lined up ready to board. There were numerous excuses as to why they didn't have their invitations but they were not being let on. There were people dressed in black that showed up and they were turned away; no Manta, no ride. People stated they truly had an invitation but forgot it. "Sorry" was said in English and "*Lo siento*" in Spanish.

Women we didn't even know were trying to get on the bus by attaching themselves with a single man. The tourists were even asking if they paid, could they come. It was ridiculous. Some asked if it was a tour, could they come. There were even vendors coming up to the bus trying to sell their wares. It was chaos. Finally we got all the buses loaded and we were on our way. The buses were top of the line coaches with TV screens for a movie, ice cold drinks and snacks...it was great. So with a bunch of us yelling, singing, and all laughing and drinking beer, away we went.

Two hours later we stopped at a beautiful resort or playa area along the water. There was a lovely cleared area very, very large with a blue lagoon. It was breathtaking with white sand and dolphins swimming in the lagoon. We had arrived, but in the time it took to drive there, the movie was still playing and of course with the movie still playing we all wanted to see the end of it, so no one was ready to get off the bus. We all just sat there watching the end of the movie for about twenty minutes. That was a long time, but the Mexicans do what is important to them at the time and not necessarily what is socially correct. The number of whites on the bus was very few, so ... we sat. Of course the driver sat and watched as well.

Fernando didn't care about anyone that wanted to watch the rest of the movie, all he wanted was me off that bus to get me to his soon-to-be bride, which I did. If you were in Canada, when you arrived at your destination, the bus would stop, the TV would be turned off and you would disembark immediately. There they all sat with four buses, some people getting off, some getting off and then back on. When our movie was over they all disembarked and away the guests went to the waiting area. Fernando of course, was panicking and trying to find me because I had to get to the room where Deedee was to do her hair, so I could try to calm her down... apparently she was anxious and in a bad state, like all brides are on their wedding day.

I aided in getting the beautiful bride dressed. Together we had created and assembled lovely floral headpieces to be given out to the bridesmaids and special guests and people important in the bride and groom's lives. The headpieces were handed out to these people just prior to the wedding. It really made for a personal and intimate touch and I for one cherish the memory of that gesture of acknowledgement. I still have mine in a special keepsake box.

When we arrived at the stage for the ceremony by the water, the dolphins were swimming just beyond the stage. The staging area for the ceremony, under a floral arch with the wedding flower arrangements and those dolphins playing in the crystal blue water as a backdrop and the rows of guests sitting on beautiful covered chairs with everyone dressed in cream colored clothing was like a picture from a fairytale.

When it came time for the wedding, our young friend Jason who spoke a few languages was asked to interpret the ceremony for the "English only" because the priest was Spanish and did not speak any English. The plan was for the priest to read a paragraph in Spanish and then Jason would repeat in English in the appropriate places. Fernando would answer in Spanish and Deedee would reply in English at the appropriate places. It went along quite well until the priest got to a paragraph that was very, very long. Jason looked at me and bent down and whispered, "What am I going to do? It's too long!"

I just looked at him and indicated to him, "Just do the best you can. Remember what you can of it and repeat that part in English," so that's what he did.

He looked at the priest and he looked at the people, then he looked at the bride and groom, smiled at me and said to the bride and groom. "Okay, this is the gist of what the priest said." To Deedee he said, "First of all you have to obey and do everything Fernando tells you to do because he's the boss of the household."

And to Fernando, "You can't cheat on Deedee and you must take care of her always for the rest of your life."

Well, the English only speaking people nearly killed themselves laughing and couldn't stop and the Spanish speaking people couldn't understand what we were laughing about because when the priest said it in Spanish there was nothing funny to laugh about at all. They had no idea why we were hysterically laughing at Jason's interpretation of what the priest had said. There was the odd one in the Spanish section that did understand and they were laughing as well. The groom agreed that he wouldn't cheat and the bride would obey him, if it was reasonable, and they proceeded to carry on with the "I do" and "I do." The wedding was truly a beautiful union. They were English and Spanish and they were kissing and the show went on.

When we entered for the reception there was manta everywhere. There were beautiful tables laid with manta and flowers. The flowers were different shades of rose and burgundy and creams with greenery. The picture was just awesome.

The food was imported all the way from Mexico City and it was unbelievable. The chefs were remarkable, they prepared the food under huge white tents and the aroma of delicious courses floated everywhere. The catering and presentation were like pictures out of a gourmet food magazine. There were candles waiting to be lit later in the evening all along the walkways and the paths to the dining area, the dancing area and also to the "*baños*". When it got dark and the candles were lit it was really the most magnificent sight I had ever seen. The music was playing throughout the evening. Before the dance band started there were traditional Mariachis playing and people singing and laughing. The dinner was incredible. I lost count of the courses. We ate way too much! The alcohol was provided all at no charge and it flowed like water, and we danced until early morning. We left around 1:00a.m. and arrived back at the Malecón around 3:00a.m. Those who still had it in them went to the nightclub and those who were tired went home happy and exhausted.

That was my experience of the wedding of Deedee and Fernando. It was a wonderful, wonderful wedding. A few months later, Fernando quit his job at Foxy's and they opened up a restaurant bar of their own.

That was the end of one chapter in our friendship and the beginning of another chapter in their lives together.

I'M NOT WHAT THEY THINK

What we show on the outside is what people think we are, but the angels know the truth of what shines within us.

I am just a single mom living in Mexico with my alimony cheque getting by with all my dysfunctional ways trying to better myself. Having my own issues plain and simple – nothing more nothing less. I have friends and family come down and visit and I take them out for a good time and they go home.

One night I was out with my girlfriend after a long day of actually working having a drink at my favourite watering hole, which is The Cage. The Cage is a nightclub on the Malecón that is very popular, the theme there is of wild animals and a couple of cages that people go into to dance and do a little showing of their wares.

The club was open till three or later depending on the demand, but I must say getting out of a taxi and seeing the line-up one block long and knowing it was a one to two hour wait to get in and I go to the front …smile… and walked in or if I couldn't get to the front, security made the patrons move and they reached for my hand and pull me in… Nice! *Real nice!* No waiting and a table to boot. I must say that doesn't come easy, you have to pay your dues and I guess I had.

Sonya and I had been there for about an hour and in walked a dear friend of mine that I had known since the first day I arrive at my second home ...we met at Chukka's Place. We clicked from the first hello and have been friends for years

I looked over the sea of people and saw my friend. He nodded and worked his way over to the table and there he stood in front of me with these three guys and he asked if he could join my table and I said, "Of course" and in the middle of my response, my girlfriend gave me a kick and a look of, "Are you nuts? Look at these guys."

Well they were a little scary... one was bald (deliberately) with tattoos all over his body wearing a black t-shirt and leathers, the other had a bandana on his head and the third one long black hair in a ponytail with sunglasses on and my goodness he was big. They were a little intimidating I guess but they were with Don and I trusted him. They stayed for a couple of hours, bought us drinks, we talked about nothing and everything. Nothing of real significance, the tattooed guy asked me to dance and I did.

They left, thanking me for having them at my table and were gone. About an hour later Don was back alone. He came straight over and said, "I have to tell you something!"

I said, "Okay. What?"

He proceeded to ask me, "Do you know who the guy with the tattoos is?"

I said, "No, just a guy, a friend of yours?"

He said, "No, not really, they were in from Mexico City for a few days on business!"

"Oh," I said,"... and?"

"Well, he was so happy that you were so nice to him. You didn't have to be and he felt you were very genuine and that if I ever needed help in any way...someone bothering you or threatening or if you were scared, to let me know and it will be taken care of. No questions asked," Don said, "I promised him I would tell you immediately so I just did."

When he told me who he was I went, "Oh my god, you are *kidding!*" I gave a big gulp and deep down I was glad I had been nice! I never did need his services, thank God, but only in PV. That would never happen in Canada under any circumstances, never mind to me, just a person with no clout or anything of importance when it comes to that kind of stuff. For that to happen - *That is scary!*

As I was sitting with Sonya going over what had just happened, a young man in his late thirties, not bad looking, blond, blue eyes, about six foot four tall, came up to the table and introduced himself as Travis and asked if he could sit down and talk for a few minutes. He was from California and his job was to protect people... I looked at him with this dumb look and said, "Oh, that's nice, and what do you want from me?"

He looked at me and said well, "I would like to work for you!"

I said, "Doing what?"

Sonya started to laugh and went to get a drink. She whispered in my ear, "I told you not to invite those three guys to our table! Now look what is happening!" she said giving me one of those, *I told you so* looks.

He continued, "I heard about the other night with all those girls and the VIP at After 8 and then at the Crystals Disco and I know why you live where you do to keep a low profile and all."

Sonya returned to the table and sat down beside Travis and told him quite bluntly that we take care of our own and we didn't need his services, thanked him and politely asked him to get lost. She looked at me and said, "For someone so smart, Sheila, sometimes you are just plain stupid or you just see the best in everyone no matter what. Maybe you do need protection!"

I said, "Is there a full moon or a Gang Convention in town or is everyone just full of testosterone tonight? My god, please check the drinks."

Never saw him again except I ran into an acquaintance a week later at Foxy's and she asked me if I had talked to a friend of hers from California and I just laughed and said, yes I had and that was the end of that conversation. I looked at her and wondered what she thought I did for a living. So most people think what they think whether it is true or not; they have their thoughts and opinions and they aren't going to change.

Sometimes it is what it is and there isn't much one can do about it, but I know that my angels are there to help and guide me when the people are not what they seem!

AFTER 8 INVITATION

*Be kind to everyone - you never know
when you are facing an angel*

For all the years I lived in Puerto Vallarta, every Wednesday night was Ladies' Night at the After 8 Club. After 8 was a real nice place inside, there were three levels. These levels started at the main bar and went in a horseshoe shape around the room. The second and third floors had very wide terrace-like walkways between each level and section. The dance floor was one step below the first level in the middle of the horseshoe with lights in the floor and strobe lights above. On the third level was a second bar that was near the stair case to the VIP section, which had its own dance floor. It was very nice indeed!

There were at least seven nightclubs maybe more, but those were the ones I went to in those days. Each club had a different night of the week for Ladies' Night so that they each had one night in the week when they dominated the attractions that would bring in the tourists. At After 8 for an eighty peso cover charge you could dance all night and drink free. If you paid your waiter fifty to a hundred pesos, after the first drink, he would make sure you got served all night long no matter how busy it was, and in all the years I was living in Puerto Vallarta there wasn't ever an empty chair or table at After 8. It was so popular you had to know someone in charge to get in, never mind get a seat or table. The lineup started around 10:00 p.m. and extended up to a block long and it lasted till around 1:00 a.m. when it tapered down to single file. The Club was open till five in the morning.

Well, I was very fortunate, I never stood in line and never had to wait...ever. I don't know why really, except I liked everyone there and they liked me. When I worked for Time Share I would always take along ten or more people. I would contact Pantera, the manager, ahead of time to tell him approximately how many I would bring and he always took care of us. When I went alone I walked in ahead of everyone and they just nodded and I went in. It was great and I soaked it up and felt very special but at the same time I felt I was trying to be humble about it...ha-ha! Some people would look at me and wonder, "Who the hell is she?" because I was always greeted like I was somebody important and never a word was said.

One day, my son called me and told me there were a group of his friends and friends theirs coming to Vallarta. He had asked them to bring a few personal items to me and asked if I would take them all out to a nightclub one night and instruct them on some of the do's and don'ts in the clubs in town. The girls were ages from eighteen to thirty, from Canada and the United States and then there was me twice the age of most of them and a couple of my local amigos.

I got in touch with Pantera and told them I had twenty-two girls coming and wanted the private VIP section where there was a security guard at the bottom of the staircase and no one else would be allowed to join us. They of course gave it to me. They had chairs and tables set up for us and everything we needed. The fifty pesos from each of us after the first drink equaled a total of eleven hundred pesos. Now you have to understand that these guys make only fifty pesos for twelve hours of work, that's five dollars...Isn't that *awful*?

This was my understanding. They worked for tips. We were being pampered and we got anything we asked for, anything, even when one of the girls asked for a guy on the dance floor below to come up and join us in the VIP section. There was also a dance floor in the VIP section so you didn't have to go downstairs if you didn't want to. Allan and his gang of guys from Canada were in town and they knew one of the Canadian girls so they came into the club and spotted us and up they came and joined us. These five or six guys had money to spare. Two of the guys were bartenders in Canada and wanted special shooters made. They proceeded to tell the Mexicans how to make them and tipped the waiter a hundred pesos with every request. The young man who was our waiter made over five thousand pesos that night. Everyone was talking about that night for weeks. What a blast, we ended up on a three day party adventure.

During those three days at the different clubs we visited, I was approached by strangers, tourists or locals, asking me, "How much?"

I replied, "How much for what?"

They answered, "How much *dinero* for one of the girls?" They seemed to think that I was a Madame or the "Queen Bee." I was boldly told that they would pay up to three hundred dollars for one of the girls for the evening. I was shocked! After laughing about it I replied, "You don't have enough money for one of my girls, none of them are for sale!" I told the girls about the offers and we all had a really good laugh.

One girl stated humorously, "The way we have been spending our money in the last three days I may have to take him up on his offer."

I never thought in a million years it would be like it was. I heard later what the young waiter made at the end of the first night at After 8 and every waiter that I knew was mad that they had not been asked to wait on us. I never thought about it at the time. I just thought he was assigned and that was that. I didn't know he was going to get paid like he did. I didn't even know at the time Allan and his friends we coming, that part was a bonus, but from that time on for years I was known as the queen – *La reina*. It never changed. I went back after being away for five years and they remembered me and I was treated the same *unbelievable way*. People would tease me and tell all the tourists that I was the Ambassador of Puerto Vallarta.

The guys at After 8 were great. There was a time when the After 8 club went on strike and those poor guys had to take turns outside the club picketing for hours. Sometimes they had to stay there all day in the heat and all night with no breaks, no nothing. I lived one block away and I would take them down food or drinks. I felt so bad for them every night I would make up eight to ten hamburgers and on my way out I would walk past them and give one hamburger or each of them a big bottle of water to share. I thought it's the least I could do. I didn't think anything of it but I guess they did. They were very good to me and always looked after me and made sure I was safe and nobody bothered me.

When After 8 reopened they gave out special invitations to a grand reopening night. Everyone wanted to go but they had to have an invitation or be with someone that had one to get in. One day I heard a knock on my door. Someone I didn't really know was standing there and he handed me an invitation. He was one of the office employees from After 8. I said, "What's this?" and he told me what it was and that he was told to hand deliver it to me and make sure I received it. He was also told to let me know that the dress code was to be all black and I would be taken care of when I got there and I was not to stand in line. He said he had to know if I was going to go because he had to report back to the office with my reply. I believe that I replied with a yes but asked him why did I get this special invitation? He said he wasn't sure, but he knew that my name was the first on the list of invitations to be made up, that there were only so many being done and that all the special ones were being hand delivered. With a big smile he told me that I was the first to get one.

The night of the opening there were literally hundreds of people there waiting to get in all dressed in black and all of them were Mexican …except me and one other blonde woman. Who she was, I don't know. She came over to me at one point and sat down and said, "What's with this you and me?"

I just looked at her and made a funny face and said, "Yeah." A sea of black hair and black clothing and her and me the only two blondes, it was a little odd! I never felt so different in my life. I really knew what it was like to be in a minority!

I was seated at the table of the mayor of Puerto Vallarta. I was struggling with my Spanglish and I asked what he did for a living and he told me he was the mayor. He told me he intended to clean up the streets of the city by eliminating the packs of stray animals and by finding homes for the homeless children wandering the beach and the streets at night. Not much more was said between us. I had a feeling he was a good man and would be a good mayor for the city.

There was a main speaker talking about God knows what, all in Spanish, a friend of mine sang a song, some traditional entertainment and then a gift of a rose to every female there.

They toasted with champagne and then the doors opened to the public and the party was on. Oh, and by the way, the mayor was good for his word: there are but a very few dogs on the streets, the odd cat in a restaurant and *no* more children on the beach or streets wandering from place to place.

I think if we care for others the way we would like to be cared for and treat others the way we would like to be treated, life supports us and our angels work through the actions that we do in our everyday living.

EXOTIC PET

A lover's kiss is like the brush of an angel's wing

When life throws us a curve that we were not expecting we must compensate. My curve was a divorce. My dream was to be together with the one I loved till the end – whichever one of us God chose to be first. I thought I would walk down a path of delightful experiences shared together throughout the years with fond memories of the good and bad times that were placed before us and, having weathered it all, look back at a job well done. Well, that didn't happen for me.

I was devastated with the shattering of my dreams and hopes. *Now what?* This is the time to get an exotic pet! I don't care where you live or how old you may be. When a divorce takes place your self-esteem is also gone. Everyone needs to feel desirable or wanted and being needed just doesn't cut it. We carry self-blame (even if it's not totally our fault) That question of, "What did I do wrong? What could I have done differently? Why couldn't I fulfill his needs?" ...all the above, and more, but it truly doesn't matter. All the reasons that make us feel better – *don't*.

I was left empty and needing to start over and get a new dream! But in the meantime, what to do about this self-worth issue! Well, for me it was Mexico – the men there are a different breed. I'm talking about some of them, certainly not all, but they are charming, handsome, verbal perfectionists in what they say, and believe me most of the time, they don't truly mean it. Mexican men in my experience say what they feel at the time and truly mean it, but it can flip in a moment. They are functioning from their emotions not the reasoning abilities in their head. They treat you like a queen, doing whatever they can to please you. Unlike the average Canadian man, in my opinion, who functions from his head not his heart. And some only function from below the belt, if you get my drift.

These are exotic pets. The rules for having one of these delightful ego boosting creatures is that they are not yours to keep and need to be approached with caution, meaning do not take everything that is said and done to heart or your heart will be broken for sure. Anyone that has had their heart broken needs an exotic pet. Now let me explain that this is in my belief and to my understanding, they are unique to you, they're not just any guy, a new boyfriend that really likes you. An exotic pet is handsome, charming, and full of many talents such as dancing; walking in such a way that he takes your breath away. He looks into your eyes and you melt or you look away because if you stare at him too long you think you will melt like a chocolate bar sitting in the sun.

It doesn't matter if you pay for him, or it just happens it doesn't matter because it's not a moral issue or a love issue it's an ego issue, and yours has to be healed and to me this kind of man fills the bill and in the end we feel beautiful, and desirable. I know that this isn't always possible and some are not in a position to get one of these creatures so other courses must be taken to bring back our wounded heart and mend it into a working functioning part of our existence again. Hope must be restored and the faith that we can find another. And most of all, that love of the self will override all the rejection we felt, the pain of feeling not good enough, whatever has been lost or taken away from you. We have to come to a place inside that tells us we are desirable and we did nothing wrong and we can love again and not to be afraid of getting hurt. And not all people will treat us as did the last one, whether it is a male or female who is the victim. Believe me that first hurt will never come again, if it does, it will never, ever feel the same or worse because that first cut is truly the deepest.

I got an exotic pet. I have to confess that it wasn't for a few years after my divorce. I think it takes a year to forgive a year to forget and a year to get your act together. Then it just happened to me. I was walking alone one day in an area where there was a new hotel being built and as I was passing by there were four men standing outside the building discussing whatever. As I walked passed one of the men took off his sunglasses and looked at me and smiled and then winked. I smiled back and kept walking, I could hardly contain myself. The one thing that a man could do to me and, I think, get anything he wanted, is to wink. I couldn't remember the last time anyone winked at me. My ex used to do that and I just loved it. I have no idea why but the most awesome thing a man can do to me is wink. There is nothing that could be said to me that makes me melt as much as that gesture.

His name was Carlo, olive skinned with green eyes that were almond shaped with a fringe of beautiful thick lashes that extended from both eyes like fans. He spoke with a deep soft voice and in English, which helped the relationship come together much easier for me. One of his talents was that he could dance and make me feel like I was the best partner on the dance floor. His wavy jet black hair was just to his shoulders (at the time this was the style). Carlos would wear it in a ponytail most of the time. My exotic pet strutted as he walked and carried himself so well that when he stopped whatever he was doing and looked at me it took my breath away just watching him approach me on the street. I would get so excited I thought my heart would beat right out of my blouse.

He had a moustache that wasn't too big, just perfect on him, and when he smiled and laughed his dimples would show then disappear as quickly as they came. His mouth was full and thick with a set of nice white teeth. Carlos had that superman chin. He was picture perfect to me. Also, he was a little younger than me, well a lot younger – around ten years. They say the rule is and I don't know where this came from but someone told me this number rule: you take your age and divide it in half and add seven years and that age is as young as you should go and anything higher is just fine. He was smart too. He installed music systems for a living.

I only saw him that once, then a couple of weeks later I was at a nightclub with a few friends and we were sitting at a table and four men walked in and sat a few tables away from us; when I looked over there he was. I smiled at him and he got up and came over to the table and said, "I have seen you somewhere before, haven't I? You look very familiar."

I said, "Yes, at the new hotel going up."

He smiled and said, "Yes, I remember now, could I buy you a drink?" We hit it off and that's how it started. We had fun for two months and one day. He was in town to install a music system in one of the new hotels and then off to the next assignment. He was gone to Mexico City and he never came back.

In the time that we were together, my self-esteem grew and myself-worth became a lot more solid. I didn't think I was a loser or undesirable anymore. I knew inside that it wasn't a permanent arrangement so when the time came I knew it was time to let go and remember the good times with Carlos with no regrets or guilt.

It was an experience I will never forget, and I remember with great pleasure to this day if I hear a song on the radio or a smell that was his I think about how fortunate I was to be given that wonderful memory and how lucky I was to have a delightful pet for even a short time. This would never have occurred in Canada for me I can guarantee you that. In Mexico, some people just live from day to day and have no hang-ups about age or station in life. They accept it as it is and when it's over it's over.

KASSIDY AND THE SHAMAN

Sometimes an angel works through the mortal form.

It wasn't a day like any other day, I was at home and not feeling very well, which was very unusual for me. I didn't get sick or get headaches like many of my friends did. My stomach was in knots around the navel area, I felt like I was going to vomit. I hadn't done anything to warrant this awful stirring inside me. I told my friend the psychic about it and she said to phone home immediately that it was my maternal instincts kicking in and there was something very wrong at home.

I phoned my son, the oldest of my three children, to ask if anything was going on there that they hadn't told me about. Sure enough, my Kassidy my granddaughter, son Jeff's daughter, was very ill they didn't want to tell me because I was so far away. Kass had a virus that had made the left side of her face paralyzed. Normally, children four years old do not get Bell's Palsy. It more often strikes people the age of sixteen or older. Doctors were treating her with prednisone, a form of steroids. It was my understanding that this type of virus sometimes could not be reversed and some people are left with permanent facial damage. This news was very shocking to me and I was devastated! All I could think about was my little granddaughter could be disfigured for the rest of her life.

Before I left for Canada, there was a knock on the door and a young man was standing there. He was wearing distinctive clothing

... Native Indian, his top was handmade out of leather, the design on the jacket had many seed beads sewn on individually in brilliant colours, absolutely beautiful and the craftsmanship was exquisite. He was wearing a headband on his long hair that was in a braid. He stood about five foot six tall. He was not a big man in stature but he was big in demeanor. This person had the facial features of someone from the Yucatan. He introduced himself, although I have forgotten his name now. He was in his late twenties, maybe early thirties, he told me he was a Shaman and he had heard about my granddaughter from a friend of mine.

He asked me very softly if he could come in and see a picture of her. I looked for the most recent picture of Kass and very reluctantly and with a shaky hand I gave it to him. He looked at her for a few minutes and said, "You must go home." He was staring at me with his black almond-shaped eyes, never once blinking and he looked at me till I answered him. I just looked back with tears in my eyes and informed him that I was going in a few days; that I couldn't get a flight out any sooner.

The Shaman told me, "I don't want you to do anything but be with her and take a walk, hold her hand and just be with her." He gave me a little leather necklace with a hand carved picture on it, it was about a half inch wide and one inch long on a leather string on each side of the object. I was to tie it around her neck, stay with her for a few days and then come back, which is what I would have to do anyway. We were in the middle of building a restaurant and I was in charge. I could only go for a few days.

So home I went to be confronted with my "little cookie," whose face was distorted with the whole left side paralyzed. My son was in a terrible state when I arrived. They had taken down all the mirrors so she couldn't see what she looked like. They told him she might get the nerves back in her face in six months or so maybe a year! I took one look at her and almost fell over. It wasn't a pleasant thing to see...I told Jeff, "I don't care whether you believe me or not but

I am going to be with her for a few days and when I leave within four days it will be gone."

He just laughed at me and started to cry, "Yeah, yeah Mom, whatever you say. You know more than the doctors!"

I told him, "No, I don't know more than the doctors but I know that miracles happen every day and sometimes, just sometimes, doctors don't know everything. Doctors are trained to take care of end effects, to deal with the problem at hand but they don't look to the cause. They can fix a broken leg but they don't know why the person broke it. It was broken because that person fell. It's called an accident!" I was expressing to him in a very loud voice, "You don't know how she caught this virus and believe me you won't know how it's going to leave! Only God knows these things ... Oh yeah, you have no faith!" I said to him, "Believe that something greater than you or me is going to intervene here!" So I stayed for three days and then I left.

A couple of days after I arrived back in Mexico, Jeff phoned me and said that the paralyzed side of Kassidy's face was working again and the doctors couldn't believe it. I just gave a sigh of relief at my end of the phone and said a few words to him and hung up. I took a few moments to thank God for my granddaughter's health and for sending me the Shaman. I never did find out his name nor which one of my friends had sent him.

Forces that can't be seen by the naked eye are always working and we only have to tap into them, whether it is just belief or an inner knowing. Whatever your belief system is we all know "Something Greater" is in our lives wanting to help us and all we have to do is submit to the unseen forces that create our world around us.

Today she is doing just fine and is growing up to be a beautiful young lady inside and out. She unknowingly had angels in Mexico working for her; there is no such thing as borders in the realm of spirituality. One day I will tell her the whole story.

SCORPION IN TEPIC

*Angels come in many forms, some have wings and halos,
others come as doctors and lawyers and such.*

I passed a lovely little bar that was a few blocks from my place, it was called the Norwegian and it was owned by a very good looking man named Martin. He was big, tall with blond curly hair and big green eyes. Sometimes there was a man there named Jorge. He was a lawyer and a very nice guy. One day he invited me and a few friends to go to his place for the weekend in Tepic. We left Friday afternoon. Tepic is about one or two hours away from Puerto Vallarta. It's a nice little village. I had never been there before and was looking forward to it.

We arrived around dinner time and went to his home, which was very nice, quite large with a lot of bedrooms. We all chose a room and got set up and went off to see the town square and church and then to a bar to have a few drinks and play some pool. Well, it started out just great. About halfway through the first game I was in the process of making a terrific shot and something hit my arm. I looked at the sleeve of my jacket and didn't see anything I looked around and on the floor, there nothing there, so I continued my play. As I was standing there waiting for Maria to take her turn and shoot, I could feel something going up my arm and I looked at my right arm and in disbelief I saw a scorpion casually crawling up to my shoulder. I of course screamed. My heart was pumping, my mouth was dry and I was just shaking. I had never seen a live scorpion before, never mind up so close. I pulled off my jacket as quickly as possible knowing it had gone under my very large collar. Everyone came rushing over and someone picked up my jacket, looked it over and said I was mistaken. I got carried away with my imagination!

I insisted that it was under the collar and I wasn't going to put it back on…it was about two inches long or more, it was beige in colour and that was that! I insisted, "I know what I saw!" So the coat stayed on the ground. Maria asked if I was going to pick it up or put it away or what …

I said, "*No way!* I am not touching that jacket ever again. Why, do you want it?" And of course she said yes, she always liked it she said the pink and silver went nicely with her black hair.

I said, "So will the beige scorpion when it bites you!" Everyone laughed and she put it on and we carried on with the game. About fifteen minutes later out from behind the jackets collar crawled the little creature and proceeded to start down her shoulder. She spots it and at the same time so did her boyfriend and he whacked it off of her shoulder and it flew through the air to the floor. We all stood there looking at it.

As it ran across the ground, everyone was having a comment like, "Oh, that's a big one, oh shit, I didn't believe you, oh well, if there's one then there's more!" And of course I am saying over and over, "I *told* you guys!"

Maria was saying, "So I guess you want your jacket back?" I assured her I didn't; I gave it to her and it was hers.

In a very concerned voice when I verbalized, "If there is one there are more." I looked up at the thatched roof and proceeded as fast as I could to leave the room stating that I had had enough pool and I was on my way to somewhere that had a different roof. "*Adios, amiga and amigos!*"

As we left the building they informed me that if I were to be bitten, the house over there, as they all pointed to it, was the one

I should get to as fast as I could! I was told to make sure I checked my runners before putting them on and shake your clothing before putting them on and look over my luggage just in case. That night I didn't sleep well. I had them on the roof, on the floor, walking along my headboard - everywhere. We left the next day around noon and I think I was the first to get in the car. I couldn't get out of there fast enough and I never went back to that place again. Many times Jorge would invite me to go and I would just look at him with a look of 'you've *got* to be kidding' and he would jump up and yell and shake his arms and mimic me to no end. They never let me forget it. I would give him a loving slap and just laugh and repeat with laughter, "No, thanks but thanks for the invite anyway."

That memory will never leave. Snakes and scorpions are not my favourite creatures that's for sure. They said they didn't know why but there seemed to be a lot of scorpions in Tepic.

TAROT READINGS

When we are closed minded we miss experiences we cannot see.

Many years ago, I would say maybe forty Christmases ago, I received in my stocking from Santa a Tarot card book and an Astrology book. At that time in my life I knew nothing about astrology or card reading ... growing up, my family didn't believe in any kind of silliness, they weren't religious in the go to church sense either. My parents were very practical and used their common sense. They were two dimensional thinkers – if you can't see, touch, and smell or hear it, it really doesn't exist and any kind of magic was just tricks you didn't understand. The type of thinking for example, if there is no cue ball on the pool table it is gone but it isn't really, it's in the pocket in potential, ready to manifest when the elements are exposed.

Getting these strange books was very exciting for me at the time, I would be very entertained. I was fascinated with astrology, being adopted I really didn't have much to fall back on when relating to habits or gestures. Sometimes comments were made that would be said about my sisters, "You do that just like Grandma." I never got that kind of feedback.

I started to understand some of the reasons for my ways, it validated many of the habits I had and other gestures that I did as an individual. The Tarot cards I could relate to quite easily. They were a tool for me to express the unsaid feelings I thought and to express the visions I saw in my head. Within a very short time, I could read the meanings of the cards quite well. I never really thought about the power in reading the cards I just did it for fun and never ever took the time to be serious, after all, I wasn't anyone with any importance in this field of knowledge and I never claimed to be good at it nor would I claim that what I said would come to be or was the truth.

When I started to read cards in Mexico it was a very odd thing. I was doing it for my friends every now and then. Most wanted it done when something awful was going on in their lives; it was never done when everything was going well.

My friend is a psychic and does her readings by holding on to something of theirs, I can't do that. It really started in Mexico when I did her cards and she insisted that I was really, really good. She wanted me to read for people on holidays, charge for it, and she would send them to me. "You have to charge for two reasons," she told me. "One of the reasons is it makes the reading important and gives it value to the client. Two, money is a symbol of exchange that must occur for the reading." I didn't really care for that but she said she would tell them before the reading how much and it must be paid before they begin the session. So I said, "Okay," truly never thinking she would get anyone. I was to charge two hundred pesos, which wasn't very much ($20.00).

I talked to my friend that owned an internet café and he said I could use his back room, so I did. I helped a friend open a Sports Bar close to my home and I started doing cards there! I had read for some young men that worked at Chukka's Place and one day a taxi pulled up to the bar and three girls got out and came bouncing into the bar asking for me and wanting their cards read. They all wanted readings for three hundred pesos each ...that's what they were told by one of the guys at Chukka's. Oh my god! I looked at them and said, "Okay, drinks are on me." I read one at a time - three hours later I had made nine hundred pesos. I couldn't believe it. Wages were fifty pesos a day.

This is a little off the track but one day a woman came in and said she would read my cigarette ashes if I would read her cards. I had never heard of that so I did. She showed me how to do it and it is very interesting; it's kind of like reading tea leaves or Persian coffee grounds.

After a couple of weeks I had to start making appointments with people. There wasn't enough time in the day to fit everyone in. It just blew me away the amount of people who wanted their cards read! I couldn't run the bar! After awhile my friend came to stay and he ran the bar. I was too busy in the corner doing readings. On my days off at home they would come or in the evenings or in the morning before work. I would be shopping or riding the bus and I would have people wanting to see me.

I am going to share two experiences I had. The first was with two older ladies from Florida that had a laundry business. They were so cute. Their heritage was Jewish. I loved their accent and that old-fashioned demeanour. It is hard for me to read two kinds of people, the very old, by that I mean by over seventy and the young, under seventeen. The old because there's not much to tell them in the future – they have done so much. And the young haven't done enough and there is so much to tell them and to influence them isn't that great of an idea especially if it's negative. The way we believe things and have certain attitudes towards our world around us is from suggestions felt or opinions believed and if those suggestions are wrong or the opinion is incorrect ...*wow!* ...I don't want that on my conscience.

Now about these two ladies, they had heard about me from someone in a clothing store down the street and they had been given directions to where I lived and came over. They wanted to know certain things that were very hard for me to answer. I told them many things that they had wanted to know but one particular thing was about a friend of theirs and they wanted to know if they should go home or not. *Well!* How do you approach something like that...first of all I said, "He is really, really sick! The number three came up indicating three hours, three days or three weeks. I said, "I think, personally, it's three days."

They made me so nervous! "You are asking things that are beyond my powers." They didn't care. They both looked at each other and then at me and said, "You *tell* us. We *know* you know!" So I told them what I knew. They paid me and seemed happy when they left. One week later she phoned me and thanked me for the information on their business that I told them about. They were very surprised with what I had said and that it was true. Their dear friend died in three days, they were glad they had left the next day for home. They had one day with him and the next day he was gone. She thanked me for that because they weren't going to go home for another two weeks and she said because of me and my definite way of telling them they believed me and did go home and they were very grateful. So there you go, sometimes it works out for the best.

The second experience or encounter was with a woman in her forties, tall and quite big in stature but not heavy just a big woman. She was from New Brunswick, Canada, she was sent to me by one of the beach boys that do the parasailing. She wanted a reading to do with herself, nothing really, just wanted a reading in general... She was bored and wanted to hear something about herself that a stranger could tell her. I said, "Okay, here goes." I told her that the young man in her home was waiting anxiously for her to return... when I told her this she said, "No, there isn't anyone in my home waiting for me!"

I said, "Well, I see a young man in his late thirties, black curly hair, hazel to green eyes."

She answered, "No, not at all."

I said, "Well, maybe it's in the future." And I just shrugged my shoulders. I told her to get back to her hotel now when I was finished, that her business was in a bad state of affairs, "Somehow, the business is good but something is wrong." She replied that everything was good that's why she had gone on holidays and everything was being managed quite well in her absence. I said some other things and she left. And I thought, *Well, that didn't go so well.* I laughed at myself and that was that.

The next day she came running into my place and grabbed me and said, "I have to talk to you! You were right, there is a younger man at my place. I denied it because I didn't want to know anything negative and I was scared to hear anything about him. And as for my business thank you, thank you! I did phone home about my business. I have a big computer store and we teach, etc. and while I was gone they were going to vote me out as president and that got stopped in a heartbeat!"

I didn't hear the ins and outs but she made it quite clear that I had "saved her butt." She gave me a very large tip and a hug and was gone. I stood there looking at the waiters and they just looked at me and laughed and went back to work as I stood there with all this money in my hand. Well you guessed it, I took the day off.

Just before I was leaving for Canada I went to say goodbye to my partner, some close friends and the staff. We said our goodbyes and off I went to the airport. Upon arriving, we found out that there was going to be a four to five hour delay, that there was something wrong with the plane, so back I went to the bar.

Having a few hours to pass, we sat looking out the bar window and commenting on all the people passing by and then one of my friends said, "Well, we do have time for you to do a last reading for all of us." So I started and the last one was my partner. He didn't like me to read for him; he said I was too spooky for him but we talked him into it anyway.

I did his reading and stated that there was going to be an accident but he was involved but not really, that it didn't have anything to do with him personally but he was going to be involved. He said, "Okay, that's it I don't want to hear anything more, stop!" So I did and I got up to go to the bathroom when I was on my way back to the table I noticed that the place was empty and everyone was outside. I went out to see what was going on and there was a man lying on the sidewalk in front of the bar and Sammie was running around getting a blanket for him and telling someone to call the police. He looked at me and said, "Get away from me! You are a witch that's for sure."He laughed and said, "I think it's time for you to go back home" and he gave me a hug.

I found out while I was in the *baño* that a taxi had pulled up to let some people out of his cab and he was standing with his car door open on the driver's side and there was a sound of a truck coming up the street. Apparently everyone heard the sound and looked to see what was coming and as this big red truck went screaming past he hit the door of the taxi and it lifted the driver into the air and he landed right in front of Sammie's front windows, and the truck kept right on going down the street.

I just shook my head and smiled and said, "I came here with an earthquake and I'm leaving with a hit and run! Well, that's all folks, *adios.*"

THE LIMON KING

An angel will never portray itself as the prince of darkness, but evil will try to present itself as angelic.

The morning started out as usual for that time of year – hot and muggy with a warm wind blowing just hard enough to lift the dust off the streets into your face, unless you had on a pair of sunglasses to protect your eyes. But most wore them to look stylish and to protect their eyes from the sun's rays.

I was on my way to the sports bar that I was a part of at the time and I ran into a friend named Helena. She was something else, a beautiful blonde, she was very smart but at times so dumb, I can't explain but I am sure I will come up with an example in this short story. She introduced me to her husband who was here for the first time. Orlando (she whispered to me that, that was his nickname) had been to Mexico but never Puerto Vallarta. He had a home in the Florida Keys and wanted one here. She had come down to buy a place and her husband had come to approve the choice of one of the abodes she had found. The house was around eight thousand square feet. His yacht was at the marina and probably just as big. He would be here for only a few days but would be commuting back and forth if he found something to his liking.

He was a very big man in stature and I think very big in the business world. I had never met a man like this. I asked Helena what he did for a living and she said, "Oh, I don't know, he grows lemons I think...not sure," she said and laughed.

I said, "Lemons or limes?"

She replied, "You know, the yellow ones."

I had seen men like him in the movies and other people had talked about such characters but never ever had I been in this situation of having the opportunity to speak to one. He was so unique and interesting that I couldn't take my eyes off of him. His conversation was not of the regular topics that I have had with rich men or very wealthy tourists.

I invited them in for a drink before I opened the bar and our conversation was very interesting indeed. Before they left to walk around the town and to meet up with the real estate person, Helena asked me to come to their home for a surprise birthday party for Orlando. Fortunately it was taking place on my day off and I was delighted to accept her invitation.

The day came and I dressed accordingly (I hoped) and arrived at their new home in a very well established area of beautifully built estates. It was a mansion or whatever they call places that you need a golf cart to get around in. I arrived by taxi and announced myself to the gate man and he let me in after opening a very wide wrought iron gate and we drove along a very long drive way with BMWs and very large black cars parked along the grass lawn. I haven't seen so much grass in PV the whole time I have been there, not even at the hotels. In front was a gentleman standing in uniform waiting for us, when we actually arrived at the house and he opened the taxi door. He helped me out and sent the cab away and then escorted me to the door where another person took me in, took my wrap and then took me to Helena.

Helena was at the pool talking to her guests. I was walking towards her and she turned and saw me and left her guests and came to me and greeted me with a hug and a kiss on the cheek and took me to her husband who was talking to a man about something and he greeted me as well with a kiss on each cheek. He introduced me to the gentleman and we had a meaningless conversation, then Helena and I left to get a drink.

As we walked to the bar area there was a waiter giving out small glass mugs no bigger than my pinky finger they were on a string and he placed it around my neck and informed me that over to the left was a table with a large display of tequila ranking from fifty dollars a bottle to two thousand dollars and at my pleasure I could sample as much or as little as I chose.

In the pool were about a dozen sombreros floating in the water; there were Mexican piñatas hanging everywhere. Over in the corner was the caterer with a display of food that I wasn't sure we could eat or if it was just on display, it was so exquisitely displayed. As time went on and it got late I could look around and I noticed there were a lot of fat old men wearing very expensive suits sitting in chairs with very young girls with long hair, blonde or very black, with very short dresses walking around and sitting on knees and sort of displaying their wares. Helena mentioned that a lot of his friends had come into town to surprise him for his birthday and were going out yachting tomorrow morning then home the next day. She invited me to join them the next morning but I went to the marina and couldn't find the yacht so I just went home.

I think I was quite relieved that I couldn't find them. I saw Orlando a couple of times after that but after that trip, I never saw him again he never came back. Helena would stay for a few months and then go back and forth. I met her for lunch one day and she asked if I wanted a shriveled up lemon and started to laugh, and then she started to cry. She said you can have him and the yacht in the marina but not the big one at home that was hers because he named it after her. I just looked at her and wondered what the hell was going on. She went to the bathroom and when she came out her nose was bleeding and she said, "I wonder how I got this nosebleed." How dumb did she think I was? She started to do lines. I didn't see much of her after a time and I knew the crowd she was hanging with - they were rich and very, very dysfunctional, which I think is a nice way of putting it. I went back to Canada and when I returned after a long visit home I heard she was not in the fancy palace and on her own somewhere. Nobody knew quite where but it wasn't good and she had gone and I never saw her again. I wonder to this day if Mr. Lemon King grew green or yellow lemons or maybe he did both!

Money is great to add to your world, many wonderful things can be done with it. But it can't give you happiness or peace of mind. That cannot be bought at any price. It's not the money that is the root of all evil it's the love of it that is. I hope you find your peace of mind Helena because money certainly didn't give you the love and happiness you were searching for, nor did all those material things. I hope one day you get what you want and truly need, my friend.

JEFF GOES TO JAIL

When bad things turn out good, you know angels were at work and very involved.

In the month of February my son Jeff and his wife Kelleigh came to visit me. I was looking forward to having them there, show them my stomping grounds and meeting my new friends and to show him that I was very safe. The day came for me to meet them at the airport.

Jeff was in culture shock, he couldn't get over the poverty and the very rich; the extremes were hard for him to comprehend. Never being outside of British Columbia, Canada, this sight was unbelievable to him. He noticed the buses immediately, being an 18-wheeler driver he just was amazed at the chromed dual stacks on the buses and the detail of the paint jobs of some of them. The way people were allowed to drink on the street. How the traffic just slows down to let other cars get in and out but they never come to a full stop! How it seems to work like a very smooth running machine, until a tourist comes onto the scene and makes everything come to a full stop and start! The way the Mexicans drove just devastated him. We spent the afternoon discussing these differences in Canada and Mexico that were so obviously other worldly to us.

This was the beginning a nightmare that I will never forget, nor will Jeff and his wife. It started with us getting dressed up and taking a cab to the Malecón to go to dinner at an Italian restaurant that I loved very much. We ate and headed off to a corner bar called Coco's where I introduced them to the waiters some of whom were my friends. We drank and danced and had a great time. My room-mate joined us and we continued on to another place called the Cage. We were there till two thirty and Kell and I wanted to go home but Jeff didn't want to go. The place was hopping and the music was rockin'. So we left and went home and Jeff stayed. Time passed and soon it was five in the morning and I was getting worried. He wasn't planning on going out for that long but he was nowhere to be found. Six o'clock rolled around and of course we were up and worried sick and in he came laughing his head off and, by the way, quite sober!

I of course yelled at him, "Where the hell were you? We were worried sick, nice way to start your holiday!"

He kept laughing and said, "Sit down while I tell you the funniest story and all true!" Jeff started by saying, "I waved goodbye to you and went back into the Cage for another Corona and to talk to some people from Vancouver that had never been there before that I met on the plane coming down." The man was in construction and Jeff and he were talking about the building going up, having a great time. Then it was time to leave. He was a little drunk, well maybe a lot drunk, he started to walk home, and well that's what he thought he was doing. He had been wandering the streets forever at least that's what it felt like, finally hailed down a cab and wanted to go home and the cabbie asked him 'where'. He said he didn't know. What was the street name? He didn't know. What area? He didn't know that either! How about a phone number? What landmarks were around that he could recognize? Didn't know that either!

So, he got the cabbie to take him to the Malecón. He went to Coco's, which was closed by then, but they hadn't put up the gates yet and my friend Paco spotted him. Paco yelled at him and asked him what was he doing and of course he didn't remember him but he told him he was lost and didn't know where I lived! Paco laughed and got a taxi driver to take him to my place. To Jeff it was very scary, no identification on him or passport, no idea where I lived and couldn't do anything! Thank God someone recognized him. That was the first night.

The next day was great. We rented a jeep and went to some tourist spots. On the way back we got stopped by the police and my friend Hector started to talk to the policía in Spanish and Jeff was saying, "We are dead ...that's it ...drinking and music so loud we are done!" The officer came over and shook Jeff's hand and had a beer with us and talked about Canada for a few minutes and gave us the empty bottle and told us to have a good time in his town and left.

We went out to the After 8 down the street that night, it being close to home so he couldn't get lost! All was good. After a couple of hours, Jeff wanted to get some more money so he went home to get some around eleven thirty. Time was passing it became twelve then one then two o'clock and finally we went home. Kelleigh was furious and of course worried. Morris was with us and I said to him, "Please phone around. Where could he be?" Well, here we go... he was in jail in town. He had been arrested for trying to buy some drugs in the bathroom at After 8.

So off we went to the jail with Morris to interpret. Nobody was allowed in or to talk to Jeff but they would allow his mother to go in. I went in and saw him. He looked awful – his face was pure white and in his eyes I could see just plain fear! I asked him what had happened and if he was okay. He told me they arrested him and handcuffed him and threw him in the back of a white pick-up and took him to jail. They took away his rings, watch, gold chain, bracelet, belt and shoelaces. They threw him in a cell with fifteen or more people, all Mexican. Nobody could speak English. He said they were taking him to the *Federales* near the airport. He wanted me to get a lot of money from home because they were going to put him away for good.

He said that a couple of the guys in the jail there tried to approach him and he just started to swear and told them to leave him alone and he put up his fists and waved them to come on! They just looked at him and walked to the other side of the cell. There was a hole in the corner to go to the bathroom and another corner empty and he went into that corner and crouched down and stayed there till morning. In the morning nobody got fed except him and his was "slop", he said and he thought he was going to throw up just looking at it. He took it and gave it to an old man that was lying in the other corner. The old man smiled and ate it all. I was told by the police he was being taken to another place and they gave me the address and told me to get all his papers and bring them there.

We got the papers and off we went. Thank God Morris was visiting me from Mexico City for a few days. I had contacted the Canadian Embassy and told them the story and where we were going. They said they would get back to me. They took him out of that hell hole of a cell and took him across town to question him. We arrived at the police office across town. It just looked like any other building, all white of course. We went in and these big, big guys approached me and told me they are talking to him and I asked if Morris could go in and help with the interpreting. They agree and he went with them. It was two hours later and he was still in the room with the door closed. I had gone back and forth by taxi four times to get more of his papers, proof of who I was and then phoned the Canadian Embassy. Four hours had gone by.

They asked him where he got the drugs and he said he got them on the beach that day, and he didn't know what the guy looked like. He said, "You all look alike to me; brown eyes, short black hair with dark skin, wearing long shorts no shirt." That's it. They told him if he said he was a user they would allow the little bit he had on him and let him go. He said, "No way, I bought it, I am not a user and I don't want that on my record in Canada." It would go against him at his work. He said he got caught, he was guilty and it wasn't anyone's fault but his own! He said, "Nobody is involved with this but me." He was stupid for doing it but he just wanted to have the experience of buying in Mexico! *Real stupid*! When we were waiting in the other room I received a call from the embassy. There was a comment from one of the *Federales* saying, "Who *are* you? A call from the Canadian Embassy… Wow!"

I shook my head and said," I don't know, I am nobody …really, nobody of importance." We were sitting waiting and getting hungry so they told us to go and get something to eat and bring Jeff back something as well. They said they would be sitting out there in the office when we got back. So we did just that and we brought extra for the three men that were there. When we got back Jeff was out in the parking lot laughing and pointing at big trucks and talking to some guys that were six feet tall, the same height as Jeff. Then along came another young man and Jeff shook his hand. Kelleigh and I just look at each other and Morris was in the office with the food and distributed it all around. Jeff came in looking much better than he did the night before. Jeff ate his meal from McDonalds and asked to go to the bathroom and he was gone for quite a while. One officer said to Kelleigh, "Here is a gun," and he pulled it from under the desk and said, "You can use this on your husband if you wish," and laughed and placed it back under the desk.

She looked at it then at me and said, "Yeah, maybe I would like to." The *Federale* told us Jeff was in the other room. He can't go to the bathroom alone, he needs an escort. Twenty minutes later Jeff came out and proceeded to tell us that as he was waiting in the other room he saw under a desk, a clear bag, and in the bag was all his stuff! He looked around and nobody was in the room or anywhere in sight, so he moved to reach under the desk and a huge iguana came running towards him from the other side of the desk. Jeff pulled back and could see it had a chain around its neck so he thought, okay I am going to grab my stuff and I will kick the shit out of the iguana if it comes close. As he brought up his foot to boot it, a *Federale* came in with a gun pointing at him and said, "Go ahead, if you think you can and get your stuff…"Jeff said he took a deep breath and reached down and got his things and the guy said with a smile, "Do you need the *baño*, senor?"

Off they went to the bathroom. He came out with his stuff and started putting it all back on. Now you have to understand that things like that don't happen ...*ever*, it just doesn't! I looked at the officer and he winked at me and just smiled. Morris was saying that he had never experienced anything like that in his life and he said, "No one is going to believe me."

They told us that the head of immigration was on his way, and Jeff had to sign some papers. It was six o'clock; we had been there since seven in the morning. We were all totally exhausted. The man came from immigration and he was over six feet tall, too. Here we were with eight huge *Federales* all with big fancy 4x4s, big guns and big attitudes, with my son in the middle of the group of men talking to them. They took him into the parking lot and came back in. I looked at Jeff and he nodded and said, "Tell you later."

The man from immigration told me they were going to leave him here in Puerto Vallarta rather than deporting him. That it would be a bigger punishment to be here with his wife than home alone till she gets back. I just laughed and hugged him. Morris said, "No matter what, do not say a word, and don't ask any questions, just do what you are told no matter what, *not one word.* The gentleman named Cesar came to the desk, called Jeff over had him sign his name in two or more places looked at us and shook Jeff's hand, hugged me and Kelleigh and said to Jeff, "The next time you go to a party invite me! *Adios amigo!* I don't want to see you again!

We left the place looking at the sky and thanking God ... nothing happened, no fine, no jail, *nada!* Morris was just shaking his head in disbelief. As we were walking and talking we passed the flea market and Jeff wanted to buy Morris something for all his help. He bought him a beautiful chess set that Morris had always wanted. As we were walking out we found Kelleigh and she was arguing with a vendor and he was saying, "Your husband took a ring and it costs five hundred pesos and I want the money!

She was saying, "What are you talking about? *This* is my husband, not that guy you are pointing at over there."

I thought, *Oh my god, what is going on around here?*" I showed him Jeff's identification and Kelleigh's and told him to call the *Policía*. I called him an asshole and told him to go ahead, just try to do that to me! I was so full of pent up energy from all that had happened. Kell was telling me that he pointed to some strange guy and was told he phoned the police on her. Finally, he said, "Okay, go, go!" and we grabbed a cab and were gone. We got home and talked it all out; took showers, had a few drinks and had something to eat and watched some TV and went to bed.

The next day they went to the beach and got burnt and I went to get my nails done. As I walked into the salon everyone was looking at me and I sat down and waited for my turn. When I sat down to talk to Mara at her station she said to me, "So ... how have you been?" And smiled at me, "And how's your visit with your son?"

I said, "What's going on?"

She said, "Everyone knows what happened to you and your son and his wife."

I replied, "How do you know?"

"She returned with the immigration guy, Cesar. His wife was just in here this morning and she told us all about a real nice young man with beautiful blue eyes that her husband had to help last night. He said he was the nicest young man that he had ever met and he would like his son to be just like him. He was very, very impressed. Your son was polite, sincere, honest and never once tried to make up an excuse for what he had done. And he never blamed anyone for his actions and didn't point a finger at anyone."

I didn't know what to say. As I was finished getting my nails done, Jeff came to get me and outside of the salon a wire fell onto the street and it made sounds of bang, bang, bang as it was hitting the pavement. Jeff jumped and Kelleigh ran inside. Oh my goodness – she thought it was gunshots. We laughed and said, "No, no just power lines."

"What else can happen?" Jeff said as we left to go home to get ready for the last night of their vacation.

When I tell people what happened they don't believe me. They say that I must have done something somewhere at sometime and it was payback. I said, "I haven't done anything of importance that I can recall." There it is again - the angels active in Puerto Vallarta.

We decided to go out to The Cage for our last night and celebrate the end of a very adventurous vacation. We got to The Cage after a great dinner at another wonderful restaurant on the waterfront and we met the couple that Jeff and Kelleigh had met on the plane. We had six buckets of Corona sitting at the bar and Jeff was giving it to everyone he talked to and we were up dancing. When I went back to my seat a young kid was sitting on it and I reached around him for a beer from our bucket. He said something to me and I responded, "Excuse me, this is my chair you are sitting on and your two friends are in my son and his wife's spot."

He rebuffed me with, "F... you lady," and my son was behind me, in a heartbeat. He stepped in and said, "What's up? Give a beer to the guy."

He answered, "*Pinche* Canadian, f... you and your mother! Well, there we went, one of the bartenders was then standing in front of us and heard everything that was said to me, and then another bartender leaped over the bar coming to the aid of his partner.

Jeff grabbed the jerk and hit him in the face yelling, "Nobody talks to my mama like that." All hell broke out. The man Jeff met on the plane was hitting one guy, Kell was up the stairs standing by an old man who was telling her to stay put or she was going to get hurt, the security guy had Jeff and was taking him outside telling him the *Policia* were coming and to get the hell out. I was at the taxi trying to push Jeff inside it; the three other young men were by then outside yelling "*Pinche* Canadian!"

Jeff was trying to get back to them; the police arrived, and had gone inside. They were talking to Kell and the old man...Kell rushed out and got into the taxi. She told us that the old man told the police to arrest the three guys; that they were wrong and Jeff was just defending his mother and so we were free to go. I arrived home with four broken finger nails trying to get Jeff into the cab and my son who was just livid. Jeffery and Kelleigh went to bed and were out for the night. The next morning Paco and I took them to the airport and it was quite a relief to see that plane lift into the air for Canada. That is the story of Jeffy in Puerto Vallarta…Paco says, "If that's one of your sons, I am scared to meet the other ones in your family."

I want to say that on all levels the police officers in Puerto Vallarta were outstanding and I will always feel safe whenever I'm in Jalisco.

The Angels in our family phylum were ever busy that week! I truly believe angels were guiding the officials as well.

MANDI AND THE SPIDER

Angels can fly directly into the heart of the problem.

–Author Unknown

Mandi had come to stay with me for a week. She took the front bedroom with a window that opened onto the side street with a big lovely tree to look at.

The second night of her arrival she woke me up saying that her face was swollen and she didn't know what had happened.

I looked at her in my half asleep look and I could see her face ...it was very, very round and swollen... this I could see without my glasses and I can't see anything without them on. I jumped out of bed in disbelief at the picture I was staring at. "You have to go to the hospital right now!" I said. So off we went, fortunately the hospital was only a few blocks away. Around seven in the morning we left the hospital with prescription in hand and some antibiotics and some kind of fluid she was to drink. They felt she had been bitten by a spider. They mentioned some foods not to eat because it could kill her if she did. I thought that was a little over the wall but they were good at their jobs so no fish till her swelling of the face went down completely.

It was now noon and she was feeling much better and wanted some tea and a bite to eat so I proceeded to make her a sandwich and a nice fresh green salad. She sipped her tea and ate her salad and then started on her sandwich and all of a sudden she jumped up spitting and gasping and yelling at me. I looked over at her and wondered, *What the hell is your problem?*

She said, "Are you trying to kill me?"

I looked at her and said, "What are you talking about?"

She threw the sandwich down on the table and said, "Christ almighty! You gave me a *tuna* sandwich!"

I said, "Yeah."

She said, "It's *fish!*"

I started to laugh, "Oh my goodness, it is," I said. In Mexico there are three staples: tuna, cheese, and ham and maybe beer. Like in Canada with its potatoes and bread being their staple I had completely forgotten tuna was in the fish family! Truly a blonde moment.

As the week went on she got much better. One Thursday afternoon Karen, one of my roommates, was taking a shower in the front bathroom. Mandi was in the living room watching TV and I was in my bedroom. She came darting out of her bathroom stark naked, dripping with water, yelling, "Oh my god, a spider, no I mean the biggest mother f....er I have ever seen."

Mandi replied, "Well, I'm not going in to kill it."

So I came running out of my room saying, "Okay, okay, I will go look and kill it." I got my cowboy boot and went into the bathroom. I looked around and couldn't see anything. She wouldn't go back in so I brought her out a towel and off she went to her room. I was standing by the kitchen entrance, Mandi was standing looking at me with that 'what the hell' look. As we were looking at each other we could hear a soft tap, tap, tap on the floor like little dog paws. We both looked down in the foyer and the biggest spider I have ever see in my life was running across the floor going towards the corner of the room where there was a small table with a plant behind it. Karen came out and headed for the sofa and was standing on it, Mandi was on the counter in the kitchen looking through the opening to the foyer at me. I moved the table and it dashed out across the floor heading for the large sofa as Mandi screamed and jumped over to the chair.

Oh my god, chaos! Then it was under the sofa. I went carefully over to it and looked under the sofa and I saw it just standing in the middle doing nothing. I talk Mandi and Karen into getting at one end of the sofa and just leaning it backwards on the back legs and I would kill the spider with my boot! Well they did this but as the girls moved the sofa spidy reared up at me and ran to the corner of the couch. I scream, they dropped the couch and headed in different directions laughing and swearing and so on.

I said, "I can't do this!" So I opened the front door and saw an older woman coming up the stairs going the floor above me! "Señora, Señora!" I stop her and told her that I have a problem …tried to explain what it was and the girls were hysterically laughing at my Spanglish and my gestures of 'itsy bitsy spider ran up the water spout.' She understood me (if you can believe that) and she said, "*No problema*," she pointed at my boot and grabbed it and went into my front room, she was looking for the spider and saying, "*Donde, donde! Aquí aquí!*" She pointed to me and Mandi to tip the couch so we did and there it was, the body the size of a beer top and hairy legs extending from its body about four inches each!

She said, "Okay, okay," lifted the boot into the air and whacked it smashing its body into pulp and it made the loudest crunch, squirting the innards everywhere. That sound will never leave my thoughts and the size will be embedded in my memory for eternity! It was awful as we watched and almost vomited, she smiled and dropped the boot and headed for the door. I stopped her and thanked her very much. I gave her one hundred pesos while she shook her head, "No …it's okay…*no problema*." I just hugged her and made her take it and she went up the stairs to wherever she was going. I went back inside to my friend saying, "It was that son of a bitch that bit you last week I know it …I know it." We have geckos in our place; they are so cute we have names for them. Well, I don't,

Karen does. With these creatures around there are no bugs of any kind, but I guess this one was a little too big for them to eat.

So there you go, three women doing nothing one afternoon and had quite a story to tell everyone at dinner that night and I think at quite a few more gatherings afterwards. I am sure the spider will get bigger and what happened will become more colourful, with each telling that's for sure.

My angels were there that day by sending me a stranger up my stairs at the most important time of need!

SOME DIE TOO YOUNG

*Through happiness and sorrow angels are
with us reminding us of their love.*

I had two close friends that died too soon. They were very different personalities and their backgrounds weren't even close to the same but dead is dead, the loss of these two young men left a hole in my world for a long time.

The first one was Fernando. His nickname was 'Apache'. I have no idea why, never did ask him how he got that name. I understand he was from the Yucatan. He was of Indian descent and with his olive skin and high cheekbones, long braided black hair and the way he walked and stood when he was talking to you he certainly looked like an apache. He was in his twenties. A Capricorn, quiet, soft-spoken and a young man of few words but when he did talk you listened.

I met Apache the very first day I arrived in Puerto Vallarta at a restaurant with my daughter Carmen. He was the waiter that served us. Later on that evening at a nightclub on the Malecón he approached our table and asked if he could sit with us for a few minutes. He started the conversation with, "I think it was fate that we were to meet and there is a reason we have come together." He said I looked different than all the other tourists he had served in the past few years. I just looked at him and didn't know quite what to say except that I was only going to be here for six more days. I looked at him and said, "Really?"

He just looked at me and shook his head. He said, "Oh, I will see you again in the near future." As time went on we talked and shared and I did move down and we saw each other on a regular basis and became good friends, sharing our thoughts on philosophy and many different subjects on which we had very different points of view.

His girlfriend was my girlfriend from work, which surprised me. They were like salt and pepper. She was so blonde, and outgoing, originally from California. Apache and Sherry were together all the time. One evening I was out with my male friend Alex and we ran into them and it was funny because we found out that we all knew each other but didn't know we were connected in this way. The four of us spent a lot of time together. I really liked Sherry and the men got along well.

He left one day to go back to the Yucatan because Sherry was going home to California and wanted him to go with her. He said he couldn't do that and begged her to stay but certain things had happened at home and she apparently had no choice and had to leave. So they parted and I think he just couldn't function without her, he pined for weeks. He couldn't work. He would get so drunk, he would drink for days nonstop. It was awful to see him in such a state and not able to do anything about it.

Apache said a part of him was gone, missing and the emptiness he felt he couldn't bear. It was so overwhelming that he was going home somewhere near Cancun.

I remember I had been back home for a few months, just before I got the phone call about his death. I was standing on my balcony with the sliding doors wide open and my girlfriend was over visiting and was sitting a few feet away from me watching TV. A big gush of wind hit me and passed by into the front room where my friend was and she yelled to me, "What was that all about?"

I said I didn't know and she stated, "There is no wind today it so hot and humid."

I said, "Yeah I don't know... strange wasn't it?" And not two minutes later I got the call from California, Sherry told me the sad news. I was lost for words. I just looked at my friend and the tears flowed.

I think of the talks we had and wonder why he would take his life. They said it was an overdose of drugs but he didn't do drugs, well he didn't when I knew him, but things change. I do know when a person loses hope and can't see any future or can't find an answer to their situation it could lead to very bad endings. Apache was so spiritual I find it very hard to believe that he took his life. I just feel there is something wrong with this picture. I look at the pictures I have of him and wonder *why?* He was very special to me and he will be missed physically in my life but I do know this, the angels are with him and spiritually he is always with me.

The other young man named Anthony was twenty-four years of age. He had a clothing shop in my neighbourhood and I went into his store one day to look at the men's clothing wanting to purchase a gift for someone. I met his wife and child and we talked and I bought some jeans and left. A couple of weeks later I was in a club called Roxy's. There was a corner that I sat in and watched the people come in and they would stop and say hi to me. One night Anthony came in and stood beside me and started to talk. He never danced; he would come in for one beer and leave.

One night he approached me and said, "Can I give you a hug?"

I said, "Sure, what's up?"

"Oh nothing," he said then he started to talk. "You know, Sheila, when you are in as deep as me there is no getting out no matter what you say or do!"

I said, "There must be an answer here somewhere."

"I have always known, Sheila, I would never make it past thirty years. I have felt it since I was very little, I just know, I truly knew when I was around ten years old." He proceeded to look at me with lost eyes and I could have cried. He hugged me one more time and left the club, so young and in such a mess. I didn't see him for a while and one day I went past his shop and he said he was moving away from here to his parents' place and he informed me he wouldn't be back and he was selling the shop. So I wished him well and left.

About two months later, a mutual friend came to see me at my home to let me know that Anthony had died and so had his father. They were in the father's back yard and the women and kids were out and there was a drive-by shooting and they were both killed. He didn't seem to know why it happened or if he did he wasn't about to tell me. All I could do was shake my head.

Everyone has a blueprint in life and our paths cross and events happen. We share bits of our lives and continue on, I hope becoming wiser for it. I am realizing that life is a precious gift to be expressed the best we know how and to be grateful for the time we have here.

I think only God and his angels know the whys and wherefores when it comes to untimely deaths. I think sometimes it not for us to question why.

HOW STAR BECAME A GROUPIE

Angels speak to us in music.

Star was a young girl I met through my son. She was a friend of his that he had known for many years. They had grown up together but I had never met her.

She came down to visit him while he was living with me in PV. She was a lovely thing, beautiful blue eyes and long chestnut hair, she could speak three languages, very intelligent but not very well equipped when it came to living on her own and when it came to men she was a little naive. But very, very nice. I liked her from the first hello. She stayed for seven days and then went home. After a few months, Gab went home too. And when he was at home he phoned and asked if Star could come and stay with me for a few months while she got orientated and she wanted to stay in PV for a while. Star wanted to find work there and experience living in a different country. So I said sure she could come down and stay as long as she wanted.

While she was staying with me I found out a lot about her. She didn't even know how to make an egg sandwich or cook potatoes – absolutely nothing to do with cooking whatsoever. I was totally amazed when I learned later on that she didn't even know how to boil water! She said her mother did absolutely everything for her from cooking to washing her clothes. To me that wasn't very helpful to her. Her mother didn't give her any tools to survive on her own! Well, believe me that was going to change quite quickly. I wasn't going to be her mother...or servant. It wasn't long when I approached her on this little problem and she told me the story of her life.

Within a few weeks she was making me dinner, and doing her own wash. Ha-ha, I also found out that she was very talented, she could read palms. When she took my hand her face changed and she started to talk and she told me things I wasn't aware of and new things to come. She also told me things in my past that nobody knew but me. She was truly amazing. We had a lot of fun reading hands and cards. Funny how people who surround you are often of the same liking. I guess the phrase birds of a feather stick together is true.

Star had worked in Vancouver in a restaurant called Cactus and she was very good at her job and it became a very positive asset in Puerto Vallarta. So it didn't take her long to get a job at a restaurant here and a very good one at that. The wages of course were not like home but her tips were great. Speaking Spanish of course helped. She didn't tell too many people that she could speak the language. It was great because she knew when they switched to Spanish what they were saying about us. Sometimes it was very amusing indeed.

One evening, we were walking along the Malecón on the sidewalk side of the road and four or five young men passed us and they gave a comment about her top she had on and I wasn't too impressed and I stopped them and told them so. I stated that that comment made to my daughter wasn't called for and they were very rude! I lectured them on politeness and voicing smut was not a very good form of respect. The verbalizing of the phrase, *"Mamacita"* wasn't very warranted either and I made it quite clear that we lived here and know the implications of that saying! They just stood there not saying a word. After I gave them a good piece of my mind we turned and walked away.

Star was glad I had said something on her behalf but she was also a little embarrassed. She mentioned how handsome they were and I was still mad and said that doesn't make it okay and it was unappreciated. She smiled at me and we carried on to The Cage. We entered and sat down saying hi to everyone and ordered a drink. As it was her day off she was glad to be the one being served. In an hour or so later we were given two drinks and the waiter said it was from that table over in the corner. We looked over and to our surprise it was the young men we had seen earlier with an apology by way of the drinks. We nodded and smiled and that was that. A few days later Star came home from work all excited and proceeded to tell me that at work those guys came in for lunch and she found out from them who they were. They were a very popular band in Mexico called Chicos and they were in town promoting their new song and they were at some restaurant that was owned by a friend of theirs and they had invited her to come for drinks after work.

Well, that was the start of a great relationship with the band and Star. She went to many concerts paid by them and she is still in touch with the manager of this group to this day. So there you go, you never know who's who so be very careful on what you say or do.

HOW TO CHANGE 100 PESOS INTO 2,469.69 PESOS

If human beings were perfect we wouldn't need angels.

It was such a great deal how could I say no. The rental car was advertised for $8.38 plus tax which worked out to ten dollars US per day. I confirmed online that there were no other charges and that if I didn't want insurance that was my choice. I then contacted Cheep o Rental by phone to be sure I hadn't misinterpreted their advertisement. They confirmed that I did not require a credit card to reserve the car for the days I wanted it. I decided to go ahead and book the car for four days of my one month vacation in Mexico. I was so excited that I had found such a great deal again.

The first time I booked a rental car in advance online for a Mexican vacation I paid fifteen dollars per day and didn't need to purchase insurance. The car was delivered to my hotel door and picked up again at the hotel when I was finished at no extra charge. However, when I wanted to extend the car rental for one more day they said the promotion was over and I would have to pay full price. I remembered that experience and this time I thought I was way ahead of the game and I would pre-book the car for four days spread out over my vacation time. I booked it online and printed out the date confirmations and put them in my travel pouch with my trip itinerary.

After twelve long hours of travel we arrived at our destination, collected our bags and passed through immigration on a green light. *Yahoo*, we made it! All we had to do was pick up our car and go to the apartment.

Go directly to the Cheep o Rental sales window; do not stop at the timeshare desk for a VIP voucher. The Cheep o Rental rep was very busy on the phone with one client and had two others waiting and in process to be picked up. We found out that now the Cheep o Rental office has moved and is not on the airport grounds. We can get their shuttle to pick us up at no charge to take us to the office to write up our contract because it is at the office where the cars are stored.

We hired a porter to take our bags to the pickup spot. Little did we know that it was only across one lane of traffic in the airport parking lot. When I offered the porter twenty pesos he looked at me with sad eyes and said, "That's only a dollar, lady." I felt so ashamed that I gave him an extra twenty to leave me alone.

The Cheep o Rental shuttle picked us up in a lovely new Nissan car and drove us across the street to their lot. We finally got to the front of the line-up at the service desk after listening to another couple try to negotiate their contract we were feeling pretty nervous and not so sure we had made the right decision. We were told there are new rules about insurance for rental cars. You now have to have insurance but there are choices about the coverage. We listened to the options. Third party liability only was coverage for the other party if we had an accident but we would be responsible for any damage to our vehicle. The premium was really low, only about forty dollars US. The credit card authorization that was needed for that policy was going to be for a total of $3,600 US. I wanted to laugh but just said no bloody way.

We were told, "Then you can't have the car." After that I was getting angry. It seemed like they were out to scam us. We were really trying to understand why it was so different from what we had been told when we made the plan was proclaimed to be full coverage at around sixty-eight dollars. It was to cover the costs if we had an accident with another vehicle or if we dented the car ourselves without any other vehicle involved. We confirmed with the agent numerous times the price of ten dollars for the rental and the sixty-eight dollars for insurance coverage, a total of seventy-eight dollars we thought. The insurance authorization for this premium because it was better coverage was only $368 US. We felt that was more reasonable even though it was not what we were told before we left home.

I asked if we would be able to pay in pesos and they replied yes, we could pay in US dollars or pesos or credit card.

We decided to take it for one day instead of the originally booked two days and we would think about whether or not we would use our later days in the month at all. We thought we could use the money we would have spent on the additional days to pay the extra insurance premium for the first day when we needed the car to take our five pieces of luggage to the apartment and do our large basic grocery shopping for the month.

We asked if we should pay now or when we bring the car back. They replied that we had to wait until we bring the car back. We would also have to refill the gas tank but we wouldn't be charged any mileage fees.

We finally signed the papers.

We turned around to go to the car and found that the car we were picked up from the airport in and told would be our car, was now gone and we would be getting a Chevy instead of a Nissan. We did the required check of the car to be sure there was no damage already on the car that might be misinterpreted as our responsibility and once again confirmed that if we damaged the car ourselves there would be no charges because we had purchased the full coverage.

We headed out for the apartment already an hour and a half late to meet the property manager who was waiting with our keys to show us the suite. We arrived on the street close to our destination but it was so dark we couldn't see the numbers on the buildings so we parked the car in what seemed to be the only empty space, locked the doors and walked across the street and asked a shopkeeper who spoke very little English if it was okay to park there. She replied, "No, no it's for taxis only." She told us our place was in the next block. We returned to the car and drove one more block; found the manager was pulling away from the front of the building when we drove up. She was angry and in a hurry saying she had been waiting for over an hour and had left a note on the door for us. She got out of her car and rushed one of us in to show us the suite while the other tried to park in the only parking space on the street in the dark without a guide to assist.

If you have ever been to Mexico, you know that the curbs and sidewalks are a little different than they are in Canada. They are very high. I began to parallel park the car and had trouble getting it straightened up. I pulled in and out a few times and a woman came out of a shop beside the car waving her arms telling me to stop and she helped guide me into the spot. When I got out of the car she pointed at the front corner of the bumper on the passenger side of the car which was on the sidewalk side of the car and showed me where I had scratched the bumper quite badly on a big rock that was sticking out of the side of the curb. It wasn't visible to me from the driver side of the car while I was parking because it was below the window level and I hadn't even felt that I had hit anything. I was devastated. I almost cried. I kept telling myself it's going to be okay because we bought the full coverage package. That was my only consolation. We dragged our suitcases up the stairs with the help of the owner and locked the door.

The next day we did the shopping and errands that we had to do, filled the gas tank and took the car back to Cheep o Rental an hour early.

Now here's the magic formula. We thought we would pay in cash the seventy-eight dollars US and turn in the keys. *Wrong!*

We were first told that the amount due was now 2,469.69 pesos. Stunned, we asked well, how did it get to be that? We have full coverage we should only be charged the seventy-eight dollars US. They said no, there was an additional airport pick-up fee of fourteen dollars plus there was a deductible of five percent of any repair costs and that was ninety dollars plus there was tax added on to everything, so the total we owed for our full coverage was now 2,469.69 pesos.

I asked how do you figure the deductible amount out and was told that their mechanic had taken a look at it already and estimated the five percent of total cost of the damage to be ninety dollars US. We really didn't have any other option there was no uninterested third party estimator involved and when we said we thought their estimate sounded pretty high they replied well it's is a new car you know.

So then we agreed to pay their price and get out.

We offered up the pesos total of 2,469.69 and were told, "Sorry, we don't take cash; you have to use your credit card." I asked to put it on a different credit card and was told no. They said, "It has to be on the same credit card that we got the approval on when you took the car."

I said, "You told me I could pay in pesos or US dollars. Now you say I have to use my credit card and you don't take cash."

She said, "Yes, because it's a holiday and the bank is closed until Wednesday. We can take cash on Wednesday but not today."

So we paid using the credit card and that is how you make 2,469.69 out of 100 pesos.

To summarize, I would like to thank my dear friend Lynda for causing a scene in front of the whole office when we rented the car and she insisted that we take the full coverage and not just the third party liability. I insisted to her emphatically that I had driven a car in Puerto Vallarta for fifteen years and never had an accident and we would be fine. She said she didn't care about those fifteen years and we were getting the full deal. So I gave in and *thank God* I did!

It would have cost me not just ninety US dollars for the deductible but $1,800 US for the full repair plus the rental cost, the airport fee and the taxes. That's one week in a five star all-inclusive hotel.

Who was my angel that day?

DANIEL MY SHADOW

Angels are around us with love and when love is awakened, there is no room for negativity.

I had been on my own for a while when Francisco was in Mexico City for six months. He wouldn't be back till the end of the year. My one son had gone home and he felt I was fine living in Puerto Vallarta on my own. I was working at a hotel in the tourist business. Angela called me in when she was really busy. I really liked working for her. It was easy for me and she paid me well. I was always at Coco's, I enjoyed going there and many of my friends were frequent customers too, so I could always run into someone during the day if I was bored. There was a very young man named Daniel that worked during the day and some night shifts. He was a very quiet person, he did his job well, but he wasn't one of those who was always after the girls or drunk on his day off or partied hard. He was just plain nice for Mexico City and was here on his own too.

One night I was walking towards the bar, he stopped me at the window before I went inside and said, "Can I ask you a question?

I looked at him and said, "Sure, anything."

He looked me straight in the eye and said very softly, "Do you have an extra room I could rent from you?"

I said, "I don't rent out my rooms."

He replied, "I know that but I want to live with you." He started to blush and repeated, "Not live with you but live at your place,"

I laughed and just smiled at him. I said "Why?"

He replied, "Because I know it would be safe and I wouldn't have to worry about anything."

I smiled, "I will think about it."

He told me, "I don't eat a lot and can cook. I would buy my own food and I wouldn't ever bring anyone to the apartment," he stammered nervously.

"I will let you know in a few days." I said.

I thought about it for those few days and decided that I would give it a try. I had no idea why I was doing this but I figured that there must be a reason that this situation was put in my path. There must be something going on in my life that I wasn't totally aware of yet. I went back to Coco's and told Daniel that it would be fine for him to move in and we talked over the rules of my home and the rent. He came over on his day off with his clothes and other things. It's funny but I never questioned him on anything. After a week it was like he had always been there. Half the time I forgot he was even there. Looking back, I think he took the place of my youngest son Trent; some of his personality was similar to that of my youngest.

When my oldest son Jeff came down for a holiday they got along great and when my son was leaving he asked Daniel to look after me and he said he would pay him to go with me at night to make sure nothing was going to harm me. I thought that this was a little extreme but that's what he wanted so we agreed and that's what happened for a few months. Once a week Jeff would phone and ask Daniel how it was going and was I fine. Poor Daniel, what was he going to say, all he could do was follow me everywhere. Most of the time he wouldn't sit with me. He would just go into the places I went and stand at the bar or the door. In time, everyone would ask me where my shadow was. Daniel got a night time job so he couldn't go with me anymore, which was just fine with me and I am sure was a relief for him, too.

On his days off, we would go out sometimes for dinner and a movie or to a bar and he would sit with me and we would laugh at the past things we did and he would mention the fact that there was only one thing he hated about me when I went out, it was the fact that when I wanted to leave a place I would leave. I wouldn't say I was leaving and twenty minutes later go, I was going to leave and I did. I left right then and there! Many people questioned our relationship, they couldn't figure it out. It was simple to us – he was my friend and I thought of him as my son. I don't think he ever thought of me as his mother. I was like a sister or just his friend, I really don't know. He has been in my life for years and is married now and all grown up. He is still a waiter and is respected at his place of work. I love to take my friends there and I know we will always have a great meal and good service.

I take the time to brag about Daniel and our long friendship.

One time after I moved back to Canada, my whole family and I were staying at an all-inclusive resort in Bucerias, my youngest son Trent went into town with my grandson to take him to his first nightclub. While he was there in the VIP section, a guy about the same age as Trent kept staring at him. After a couple of hours Trent went up to him and asked him what his problem was and he just looked at Trent and said, "Are you Trent, Sheila's son?"

He replied, "Yeah, who are you?" Daniel explained about Jeff, his brother and my son remembered him from a long time ago and of course he dragged him to his table and drank Grey Goose vodka to the early morning. Daniel hadn't seen me for a couple of years; we had lost touch with each other because he was in Mexico City when I moved back to Canada. Trent insisted that he come to the resort and wake me up. This is now around five a.m. Daniel had a car and drove Trent and Jordon back to the resort. I was sound asleep but the banging on my door stopped that in a hurry, with Trent yelling, "Ma...Ma wake up! Guess who I have here!" When I answered the door I couldn't believe who was standing there. I was so happy, tears filled my eyes. We talked for a while and Trent went to bed as now it was around six in the morning. Daniel insisted that I get dressed because he wanted me to meet his wife and family then take me to breakfast at our favourite place in town. We then went back to the resort where seventeen family members met Daniel for the first time. We spent the afternoon in the sun. We had a beautiful dinner listening to live music and sharing old times and talked of the new things that were happening in his life and mine.

Daniel doesn't want to come to Canada. He loves his home and his country but he said maybe one day he will come to visit me and I plan to make sure it happens. With the communication we have today on the internet I will not lose him again.

An angel intervened that day. I believe we were meant to be in each other's life. To this day I don't know the answer "Why?" I feel something greater than him and I brought us together.

ALLAN AT CRYSTALS DISCO

Friends are kisses blown to us by angels.

—Author Unknown

This story is about me and my then new friend, Allan and now my oldest male and closest friend in my hometown. He lives one block away.

When I had my sons' girlfriends down in Puerto Vallarta on holidays we had gone to After 8 and we had the VIP section. While we were there, Tara's good friend Allan came with the guys from Canada but he stood out a little differently than the rest, he was older than them and he had a body guard that stood close to him but at a distance if you know what I mean, and he was a big guy with a short beard, curly hair and a body of a body builder. I didn't quite know why but at the time I didn't really care. I asked Tara who's that and why the guy with him, she just laughed and said well, that's Allan. Allan was big too but he looked completely different than Harry. Allan was completely bald, which was on purpose. To me he was drop dead gorgeous! He was dressed to the nines. We were introduced and the party was on. He mentioned that he wanted me to go to Crystals the next night and we would be in VIP with him and it was on him; to wear my cowboy boots and a dress. I looked at him and said how do you know about my boots? He said it didn't matter how he knew but would I wear them. I agreed and we would meet at ten, with anyone else that wanted to come.

He wanted us there for the new light show that was being performed for the first time. I said we would be on time to see the show. The next night four of us went to Crystals. We arrived around ten, when we got to the front door a very good looking man came up to me and said that they were waiting for us and to follow him, but just before we started to follow he turned around and picked me up in his arms and carried me in and over to the VIP section. I started to laugh and asked, "Why are you carrying me?"

He looked at me and said, "I have my orders." Everyone was staring at us. I was being carried and the girls were following with each of them on the arm of an escort. We get to our seats and I sat with Allan and Tara sat at a different table with Harry and the girls. We watched the amazing light show and had a few drinks and Harry was videoing the whole thing. As the time went by there appeared some Chinese girls on the dance floor and Allan was taken with them and we were all ignored so I turned to Tara after half an hour of just sitting and waiting I gave her the nod and we were out of there. She said, "You can't just leave."

I looked at her and said, "Watch me." So we left with Allan and Harry on the dance floor. We left saying goodbye to the manager that carried me in and taxied to the Cage. We were there for maybe an hour – not long – and in came Allan and Harry. He looked at me and I stared at him without a smile as he approached my table and he said, "May we join you?"

I said, "Sure, why not?" We spent the rest of the night dancing together. What had happened was never brought up nor mentioned.

He left the following day and I didn't hear from him till one day I was at a lawyer's office and I met a good looking Italian that was also in need of a lawyer and we started talking and I invited him over for a drink. He said he had to meet a friend but could he come over as well and I said sure because I had a roommate and that would be great. When he came over his friend was Allan. I almost died when I answered the door. He looked at me and started to laugh and said "Well, well, well, small world."

You must be careful what you do, you never know who knows who.

We called Tara and she came over and we had a great time talking about our holidays. I went out with him for a long time and then came a time for a commitment and he didn't want to so that was that. He still lives close by and we keep in touch with birthday calls and the odd catch up call but that's it. Always friends but never holiday buddies. He is still single and so am I. What a waste of years, I think. I believe it could have been good.

Our angels know more about what should be in our lives than we think we know.

NOBODY HAS CONTROL WITH 49%

*If you walk the straight and narrow path
you won't need the help of angels.*

We had the restaurant/sports bar. I was in charge of getting it changed from a pizza/taco joint into a sports bar. Mandi was Sammie's girlfriend and she had moved down with him to PV. She and her daughter were living with Sammie. They had been living together a lot of years but no marriage insight, which I could see. Sammie was the money man of the bar. Sammie bought a condo in Mismaloya, had some property in another small town just outside of Tepic and the bar. She was saying one day that she had forty-nine percent of the business and that she would be fine if she and Sammie broke up. I looked at her and said, "No, you wouldn't have a thing young lady, because forty-nine percent means nothing here." She got quite offended and said I was full of it! We had been drinking sangria and were well on our way to talking straight up, so I went on and on about, "Forty-nine percent means nothing. Don't you get it? You get nothing..."

Well, I went on and on...telling her I was in business with a partner and I had forty-nine percent and I didn't have any say in anything and had no power whatsoever. The people with the majority shareholding have the power, and do as they please and there is nothing you can do about it. We argued for an hour, we ended up in another favourite watering hole called Carlo's and on we went again, Mandi saying Sammie wouldn't be like that and I sputtering nothing but garbage.

I just shook my head and declared, "Watch and see, mark my words." She got so mad and frustrated at me and I just added fuel to the fire as I sat on my stool, playing with my drink and shaking my head. Mandi told me to shut the f--- up or she would punch me! And she gave me a push and pushed me so hard that I went sliding off the bar stool onto the floor! I was still holding my drink, looking up at her with my glasses half on my face and half in my hair, wondering what the hell happened. She reached down and pulled me up and we both began to laugh and hugged each other. We looked around for Fernando who was sitting beside me when this all started. He had moved away from us knowing that something was going to happen with two drunken women and neither one of them getting their point across. The bartender even stopped serving us or standing in front of us as he usually did. As she was helping me up with my glasses still crooked on my face and I struggled to stand, she started laughing again and so did Fernando and I stopped the talk and we all went to dance and that was that. We never spoke of it again but I will tell you this that when they did break up for good she didn't get forty-nine percent. She just looked at me and I just looked at her and she said, "Yeah, yeah, forty-nine percent means shit!" He did give her some money but not what she really thought she should have got.

Our angels do not do our thinking for us nor do they fix things, they do aid us in learning to understand our mistakes and learning from them.

CROSSING THE LINE

We shouldn't stop looking for angels because there is no scientific proof of their existence.

My daughter had just been married to a nice young man named Scott, he had never been to Mexico and I thought it would be a wonderful experience for them. I gave them a honeymoon holiday to Puerto Vallarta, at an all-inclusive for a few days and the rest of their stay with me. We had set the date for them to come down and I told the world they were coming.

They arrived at the airport with me crying and waving like a crazy woman. We gathered up their luggage and took a cab to the hotel. They stayed there and did the touristy things and experienced the bartering at the flea market, got their trinkets and souvenirs. One night we went to Foxy's and the band let Scott play the drums for a few songs, he was very, very good. They also got a tattoo each, Carmen on her shoulder and Scott on his ankle.

The night before they left we had a party for them and had invited a lot of people, thinking maybe sixty percent would show up. The party was going quite well, the comings and goings of my guests was wonderful. I was amazed that most of the people that I had invited came. The music was great and we danced and sang and told jokes.

Just before I felt it was time for everyone to leave, my girlfriend surprised Carmen and Scott with a wedding cake she had made herself. I was delightfully surprised as well. They each said a few words and cut the cake. Scott cut and Carmen served. But something was *wrong!* After a few minutes, everyone started to laugh and talk a little strange and I couldn't figure out what was wrong. While I was trying to understand, my roommate came in the door, she had to work late. Karen came up to me and said, "I just saw Roger leave and he seemed so confused! By the way, I thought you didn't allow any drugs in our place!" I looked at her and said quite sternly, *"I don't!"*

She said, "Well, you do now!"

I didn't know what to say and I said, "Nobody took any drugs here!"

She said, "If no one did drugs why is everyone high? Except you?"

I said, "I was the only one who didn't have a piece of the wedding cake!" Karen walked up to my friend and asked her if she had put some drugs in the cake and she replied laughing, "Yes I did, isn't that funny, a real surprise cake wasn't it?"

Karen started to scream at her calling her names. While she was leaving she grabbed her coat and her husband and ran out the door. I ran out to the balcony, I saw that they were getting into their car. Karen was so upset and so was I but more so when she told me that Roger was in NA and only three months clean and now he had to start over but she hoped that this incident wasn't going have him start up again. She hoped he was on his way to see someone in the program. This horrible act unbeknownst to all of us wasn't going to hurt others as well.

The next day we all talked about what had happened and everyone felt badly about Roger. I tried phoning my friend to talk about it but she never answered the phone and I never ever saw her again. Believe *that!* I was told she and her husband moved to Mazatlan a week later.

A few days later Roger came to see me. I hugged him and apologized and said how sorry I was about what had happened and I made it quite clear that if I had known about the cake…He stopped me in the middle of my babbling and said so softly, "I know, Sheila, I know, shit happens and I'm okay. I saw my sponsor because I truly didn't know what was wrong with me and everything is fine. I came to meet Carmen and her husband and I wouldn't have missed that. I must admit that I did feel very safe coming here because I knew that there would be alcohol but that would be it. I know you wouldn't be a part of anything that would hurt anyone."

He is married now himself with a couple of kids and doing very well and is still in NA. God bless him.

I wish I could have spoken to my friend about what she had done, I know Roger has forgiven her for her thoughtless act, I know she didn't do it intentionally to hurt anyone.

Angels were looking after him that night. I know Roger and he is thanking God and making the sign of the cross on his chest that's for sure.

KIDS ON THE STREET

Children are expressions of angels, you just have to love them.

When you live in a place for a time, especially tourist towns, things happen every day that look one way to the tourist and look completely different to those who see it every day.

I want the reader to understand that this was the way it was when I was there. Things are different today, this could have improved sooner but it didn't and it got worse before it changed. The people that governed the state and the people who ran Puerto Vallarta did nothing but ignore the problem and then one day a new mayor was elected and it was made good.

This story is of my experiences with the kids on the street and on the beaches and in the garbage dump. There were three or four different kinds of children that wandered the street at night. There were the flower children – mostly little girls between the ages of six to ten years of age. They dress really nice with their hair done so cute with big smiles going to the windows of the bars and walking through the restaurants selling roses for twenty pesos or more if they can. The Chicklet kids that are really young with ragged clothes are not so clean. These for some reason, seemed to be boys four to six years with their mother standing close by looking sad and hopeless with a baby on one hip taking anything the tourists would give them for a package of gum.

I would buy if I wanted some but it was no with a shake of my head if I didn't. I have seen those little girls go around the corner and get into a brand new van with the father, I am assuming, telling them to get in the back. The tourists wonder as I did where are the parents, what are they doing out at this time of night. In Canada or the United States that would not be allowed for a minute! Your heart goes out to them and you buy. Never ever did I see a parent standing guard as they walked the streets at one in the morning other than the Chicklet kids! I was told by many locals that these kids come from homes that are lovely and the families are very well to do. I don't know this for a fact but that's my understanding.

Then there were the older street kids, the ones in their early teens maybe twelve to sixteen. They lived on the street and slept there or the beach kids that would leave the beach around ten because they weren't allowed to stay. Where they went I never did find out. One of my friends befriended a boy from the streets and he paid the single mother to let him stay with them to go to school and have a better life and she agreed and he grew up to be a very nice educated young man and is doing very well in the business world today. His life is still a little chaotic but much better than before. Some just don't go to school because they just don't have the money. They survive the best way they know how.

When you live here, you get to talk to these kids and find out the whys and how they exist the way they do. I would bring hats and t-shirts back from Canada when I went home and I learned to just give the one shirt because if you gave them two they would sell the other one. There is always your favourite and you end up doing what you can to make his life a little easier. I watched a young man grow up and I started helping him with a reward system...If you go to school, I will give you this. If you show me your report card or your grades I would meet him and give him lunch for school or scold him or hug him. I never knew from one day to the next if he would show up. He was in grade eleven and then he was gone - just gone. I would look for him for days. To this day I have no idea what happened to him. He just vanished into thin air.

I had heard that there were hundreds of kids in the garbage dump. I don't know for sure. I never saw this for myself but I understood that they were there.

Some of the beach boys were used as sex toys. They would be on the beach by day and I understood from some of them that talked to me, that they slept in the woods at night. As they walked past my home I would give them blankets and bottled water and food, runners and shorts. Then one day they weren't there anymore and I heard that someone gathered them all up and got a place for them to live and go to school.

Mexico doesn't like do-gooders...they tell you to go home and look to your own people and clean up your own back yard. So you just kind of do it as you go. My girlfriend Lisa worked as a volunteer at an orphanage and she would get so frustrated, they would run out of paper or pens and there were no funds to get anything.

One of my favourite stories was about a young man that was on the streets doing nothing really and my friend from New York who worked for a model agency spotted Sergio and was smitten with him. To make a long story short, she took pictures of him and I still have some of the proofs today and she took them back to New York and they liked him so she sent for him and he went and was a very successful male model for years. I kept in touch but I haven't heard of him for maybe ten years now. I hope he has done well!

We can lend a hand and help even though we know we can't change the world. If you can help just one person and everyone just helped one person ...wow what a difference that could truly make.

Angels work in our lives to bring about the best, we only have to be aware that things happen for a reason...sometimes for the good and sometimes it seems for the not so good. Only time will reveal the true purpose.

CANADA DAY IN PUERTO VALLARTA

Positive acts are expressions of angels.

In Canada, July 1st is a very important day to most Canadians. We celebrate our independence with pride. There are flags displayed on our cars, flags with the big red maple leaf waving in the wind, placed on the lawns and in the windows of our homes. In the evening, there are organizations that display fireworks show. There are many Canadians that lived in Puerto Vallarta and they all seem to come out of the woodwork to celebrate this very special day. The parties did take place in every restaurant, sports bar, or clothing store that was Canadian owned. These gatherings went on all night long.

There was a tapas bar on what we call restaurant row that celebrated the biggest July 1st ever. People come from all over to party there. Usually, we give our staff the opportunity to work for Snack Shack for that special day. The amount of people that show up was always so overwhelming, they couldn't serve them all. The waiters paint their faces with the Canadian flag; some wore white t-shirts with red shorts. They served drinks that were red and white all day. Canadian paraphernalia was given away. The Canadians mocked the "Eh" verbally over and over. It's quite a sight to see and be a part of. Nina, one of the owners was a great singer and she would sing with her band that evening and there was standing room only and that included having people outside on the sidewalk looking in through the windows patiently waiting to get into the place.

The two owners were two young ladies in their thirties, also they were sisters, gorgeous blondes, and we nicknamed them the Gabor sisters. Nina worked the bar and served drinks and waitressed. Brenda cooked and stood at the door. When Brenda was on the door, people would stop and take pictures of her, she was so beautiful. We would tease her that it wasn't the tapas she cooked that brought the people in it was her looks. She would blush and walk away. Men would come in and buy a drink and just watch, enamoured with them. Nina was the brains of the two. She handled the money and the business end and Brenda was the expert in the kitchen so everything was covered, they were a great team. When we closed up the bars we would meet around two a.m. and head off to Foxy's. Without fail they would get Nina up to do a set. She always did even when she would comment to me, "Damn it, I am so tired," she would smile and do what she loved and did best.

The day after July 1st, I read her cards and I told her she was going to marry a very tall American with blue eyes and long blond curly hair. She made it quite clear she didn't like blonds and that would never happen. You know it did, about a year later. I met him and he is quite a guy. He was a computer expert and a very talented musician, a keeper that's for sure. She did keep him and in time they were married and they are still in Puerto Vallarta to this day. They opened a new business and are doing very well.

As for Brenda, she fell in love with a nice Mexican, married, had three children and lives in British Columbia. They are very happy and life apparently is good. Brenda and her family do visit her sister in Puerto Vallarta, and maybe celebrate Canada Day with the angels that watched over them while they grew into their new lives.

TAXI DRIVER GABRIEL

We are to angels like coal is to diamonds.

Gabriel was a young man around twenty to twenty-five at the most. He wasn't a talker, he said very little now that I think about it. He would ask where you wanted to go and then that was all. If you asked him a question he would answer but he didn't open up any conversation on his own. He always had a smile on his face, was clean cut, his eyes were always so clear. He was groomed with the latest hairstyle that the kids of the day were wearing.

I met him one night at a club when I needed a taxi and he drove me home. I liked his aura and I ran into him three or four times at the grocery store. One day I was downtown at the bank and he was next in line to cab someone and I asked him if he did personal taxi driving. I needed someone to take a tourist all day and would he be able to charge a certain amount and be with them as a tour guide for the day and he said yes he could do that, it was his cab and he could do what he wanted. I used him for special expeditions that came up and to take my special friends here and there. It was good for him and so easy for me because he spoke English and was so easygoing in his personality that everyone that hired him for the day couldn't say enough good things about him. After a while he made it quite clear that I was his customer and I made it quite clear that I would only ride with him if he was available that day or night. I had to wait for him sometimes because he was in the queue and if he was five or six taxis down the line the other drivers didn't like me taking him out of order so I would wait for him to get to the front of the line and in those days it didn't take long.

This only worked in my stomping grounds. The taxi drivers had areas to line up at they could drive anywhere but they had a home base that they had to queue from.

The cabs were numbered from zero one to 998 the last time I looked, I am sure it's much higher now. The zones are quite clear. If you crossed a zone by one car length it was twenty pesos and that charge could be used for one block or the five mile zone. It didn't matter, charge is done by zone not mile. At home, as the wheel turns so does the meter, not here, time or distance has nothing to do with it.

You could barter your ride back then but now there are set prices and everyone knows it. They have charts now with the prices on it to show the tourists. This is good and bad depending on how you look at it but when you are living there, different rules come into play.

Mexicans can be very possessive and when they claim you for any reason such as a client in a store you shop at lot or a place you eat or where you like to sit in a particular area you get the same waiter and by God if you get switched they have you moved in a heartbeat. Well, that's how it worked for me. I guess if they didn't like you or you weren't a good tipper maybe they wouldn't care where you sat.

Gabriel became my driver. It started with, "Are you on tonight?" and he said yes, it was his night shift, eight to six in the morning. I said, "Good, drop us off at the Cage and would you pick us up at three? Tell the guy at the door you are here for me and he will come and get me."

He agreed he would do this, and it happened a lot because all the guests I had down from Canada needed rides everywhere. After, they would just let him come in and get me. The taxi drivers are not allowed in the clubs, I don't know why! It was easier for him to come in and get me and go to his cab and wait till I went outside. He would tell me where he was parked and I would tell him the drop-off places for my friends or clients. When it was busy it was great. I would tip well because this kind of service is rare. I left my purse on the floor one night and he brought it back everything intact, not one thing out of place and I had a lot of stuff in it – some earrings to business cards. I would trust him implicitly he never took advantage of his riders ever and all I ever got was praise from the tourists that used him. *Nice kid!*

On Ladies' Night he would have to drive us to two or three different spots and he dropped off picked up and patiently waited at each place. He was great! Sometimes I would flag him down and ask for a special rate for my friends for the day and he would be there on time. He would do what we wanted and do a very good job. He would come back and take us all downtown for dinner on his last ride at the end of his shift. He would do me favours on his day off, and my friends would tip like they do in Canada and he was smiling and looking at me and I would laugh back and say, "Take it, it's okay! You did well, you deserve it." He made more in one day in tips than he would all week driving and why not? He was good to me.

I went home to Canada for a few months and when I got back I tried to find him and no one knew where he was. Without a last name I guess I wasn't meant to know anything and I have never see him since, nor do I think I ever will. I lost a good driver and a nice person who was in my life for a very short time but it was a good.

My angels I think put Gabriel in my life to make my work a little easier.

DRUGS IN YOUR DRINK
– WATCH OUT

*Those who believe in angels often are
protected from possible danger.*

The place I chose to live in Puerto Vallarta was in the area they called the Romantic Zone, it was in the older part of town. At the end of my street there was a wonderful nightclub called After 8. There were four big disco clubs in Puerto Vallarta according to the tourist guide books. The number one choice was Crystals; it had the most intricate light show I had ever seen. The second choice was After 8, the third was The Brick, in the marina, and fourth was called Gems and was close to the airport.

Spring break was a wild time in this town, the students came in droves, and we called them "Gremlins" because they would wonder from place to place in packs. The After 8 Club is the first place they would go, it was the most popular. The Club had "bubble night", which was very unique. The bubbles were solid foam and clung to the tourists like glue. They would leave the club with beer in hand and foam from head to toe. They would walk down the street leaving bubbles along the way like Hansel and Gretel and their pieces of breadcrumbs. It was a sight to see. All the students came to get information on what was going on in town for the rest of their stay.

One night I went to After 8 when it was full of students. I was given a drink by someone at the table next to me. We were dancing and having a swell time but something was *wrong*. I didn't feel the same after drinking a part of the drink that had been given to me. I was feeling odd; I can't explain the feeling that came over me. I am not a heavy drinker and usually two or three drinks were my limit. I never felt like that before. I decided to leave but I didn't want anyone to know what my real intent was so I said I was going to the bathroom. I left the table saying I would be right back and down to the powder room I went. The exit was a few feet farther, so I just continued to walk towards the door and I bolted.

As I was walking home it felt like it was taking me forever. I couldn't seem to get to my home. I was putting one foot in front of the other but my place looked like it was miles away, like looking in a pair of binoculars backwards and I was never going to get there. I started to really concentrate on my strides. Finally, I was at my door. I put the key in and that's all I remember. I woke up the next morning with my cowboy boots on, my hat at the top of the bed, my clothes still on and my purse on the floor by the bed. I jumped up wondering, *What the hell happened*! I was alone in the house at this particular time with nobody to fill in the blanks. The morning passed and as the day went on I was feeling better but still so confused. Just a blackout in my memory.

My friend Nadine came over in the evening for a cup of coffee. She also wanted the gossip on how my night went. I told her my story and she said, "Well, that's why I am here!" She looked at me with her mouth wide open and said, "Have you see the afternoon papers?"

I said, "No, why?"

She told me that her friend from Chicago went to After 8 last night and woke up in Guadalajara, completely nude in some stranger's front yard. The police come to her aid and gave her some clothes and got transport back to Puerto Vallarta to her hotel. She had no money, no purse and all her ID was missing! She had no idea what happened, or how she got there nor with whom and apparently never did recall any memory of it. There was a drug going around called "date rape", you drink it unknowingly and *whammo* ...

I was looking at my friend thinking, *Oh, my god! Did that happen to me?* My angels were looking after me, of that I was sure. That was a wake- up call for me. It was the last time I took a drink from a stranger. A lesson to learn and thank God it wasn't learned the hard way.

So be careful when you are around a lot of people you don't know. Keep an eye on your drink. I never heard of this drug happening in any other club after this incident. But we must be very aware of the goings on when you are out drinking and playing. It could happen so fast, be careful and be safe don't trust blindly, not everyone is as nice as they seem.

A BITCHSLAP TURNS INTO A HUG

Women are angels without wings but sometimes we fly on a broomstick.

I can't truly remember how I met Karen but all of a sudden she was my friend and she was living at my home. She was an odd character indeed. She was very tall and slight with very long legs, she walked like a model, you know that walk when the legs are more forward than the torso, as well as her shoulders and head. She wasn't very attractive in the sense of 'my god she's beautiful' nor did she have any outstanding features that were lovely. I must say that she did have nice eyes. Her hair was unique as well, long and very curly and blunt at the ends but it appeared to be overmuch, for her head looked like a triangle shape like God had extra hair and just plunked it on her. She was a bartender and was very good at it. Things would happen in her life that in my eyes were very strange, for instance, she got fungus under her nails from squeezing so many limes and had to wear gloves to protect her fingers. I knew lots of bartenders and not one of them had this happen to them.

I would go to Canada quite often and she would look after the suite for me and pay the bills, but when times got hard for her and she couldn't pay her share, I would let it go because it was my home and I was ultimately responsible for the place anyway. This was my way of justifying not having to confront her with her inability to carry her weight, so to speak. She also thought she did everything around the place and in fact she did her room and that was it. She had no boundaries and would cross the line and I would have to put her in her place by reminding her that it was my home not hers. She was soft-spoken and very easygoing in general and I liked that she would do anything if I asked. It never occurred to her to do it on her own but that was Karen.

Very rarely have I really wanted to hit someone. I have been truly mad and yelled my head off. My ex said I really didn't need a gun or knife – my tongue was a weapon on its own. I could cut someone up with a lash of my words and I guess that's why I have never really needed to punch or hit anyone. I never hit my children not even once. (Looking back, maybe I should have!) I have given them an open-handed slap on their bottoms on occasion. I just don't believe that hitting is the answer. I was never hit as a child, punishment was experienced in the taking away of something we loved or wanted to do. There was one time in Puerto Vallarta that I really, really wanted to punch someone in the face and would have if Mandi had not stopped me.

To this day, I still would really like to have done it. If the truth be known just thinking about it, those old feelings start rising inside me. I don't think it will ever happen again, but you never know until I come face to face with another event that would trigger it once more.

This is the experience that aroused this uncontrollable need to hit another human being.

Toward the end of my very long stay in Puerto Vallarta, which started out to be only six months and turned out to be over ten years, I was selling my belongings and getting ready to return to Canada. I was staying with Mandi at her apartment because I had moved out and had a few days to get rid of the last of my things. I had sold my TV, washing machine and beds. The rest of the furniture had been mine by rent only but I had bought the propane tank, which cost a lot and I sold it plus all the other articles that weren't part of the rental agreement. Microwave, toaster etc. – you know all those electrical things that make life a little easier.

My so-called girlfriend that had taken advantage of me for years by not being able to pay her fair share for food, phone and utilities and by living in my suite for nothing when I had to go to Vancouver showed her true nature. To me this is so funny when I look back on it! My kids were afraid of the Mexicans taking advantage of me and in my own back yard it truly was a Canadian that was the worst. To top it all she had stolen my boyfriend while I had been away! There is a lot I am leaving out in this story but I guess you can't take anything away from you that is truly yours! *Right!*

Well, she went to bed with him, and I might add she took great pleasure in telling me how sorry she was that it had occurred. I politely told the S.O.B. boyfriend to get the hell out and her as well. She did and for some unknown reason felt like she had won something. You know when someone can do that to another they will do it again and again. In the end she was hurt more than I had been. I was leaving, so Karen got together with someone else. I knew she would have to find someone real quick, she had cut her ties and had bitten the hand that had fed her and had to find another one to look after her...and she did... they decided to take my suite (which I found out through the grapevine) and she was very smug about it. She went to see the place after I moved out. Karen told everyone I knew that she wanted to see how clean the place was because she was the one that always cooked and cleaned and I did absolutely nothing!

Everyone laughed at her because that was so far from the truth they just shook their heads and said nothing. She went to the apartment and there was nothing in it. Absolutely empty! She was furious when she walked through. She thought the furniture had come with the place and it did when I rented it but the landlord raised the rent and took the rental furniture and they make it very clear that it would not be rented again furnished. I agreed to let them know well in advance when it came time for me to leave. I would get my things out and leave what was theirs. The place was bare. I even took the pictures off the walls.

One evening in El Toros, Karen came in where there were about fifteen of us all sitting around talking and saying their goodbyes to me, there was even people crying, believe that! I was so touched…I couldn't image anyone crying because I was leaving. I wasn't crying but they were! I was sitting on the inside of the table and Sammie is on my right and Mandi on the left and people all around the table. In marched Karen and she's just bouncing. Her hair was going up and down as she is about five eleven in stature and I was a little five three and a quarter. She walked up to the table. Her face was beet red, her eyes just glaring and her hands clenched and on her hips. She was cursing and yelling, "You *bitch!* How *dare* you take everything!"

I stood up. I had had it! Enough was enough. I said to her, "If you don't get the hell out of here right now, you will live to regret it!" I stood firmly leaning up against the table. I was shaking and I closed my hands and started to bring up my right hand, which is now a fist and am white as a ghost (so they said later).

As I was standing there Sammie says, "*Sit down,* Sheila! Forget it, it's not worth it. *It's not worth it!*"

I paid no attention to his words and now I was ready. One deep breath and wham – she's going to get it! All of a sudden Mandi is yelling at me saying something, I didn't understand or know why. I was in my own world…she is tugging on my arm and I turned to her and yelled, "*What!*" And I just looked down at her… She said later my face didn't even look like me! It almost scared the life out of me! Mandi had never see that side of me before, everyone around us went quiet …the whole place was in silence, the music even stopped, the waiters had stopped doing their job. Apparently the owner came out of his office and his wife in the cashier's booth came running to the table. The bouncers were standing beside Karen on the opposite side of the table wondering what's going on and waiting to see what was going to happen next.

As I brought up the right arm, Mandi stood and stopped me with her body and grabbed my body and pushed me down and reached across the table and grabbed the front of Karen's sweater and said, "Get the hell out of here before she kills you!" Karen said a few more f....words and left. All of a sudden I am back into reality and I turned to Mandi and sat down again. Everyone started to talk, the music starts up and away we go with the evening.

I said to Mandi, "Why did you stop me?"

She replied laughing, "Well, I saw your face, saw your fist and knew she was going to get punched and if it connected, we would be out of here in a heartbeat because she would be on the damn floor and Policía would be everywhere and I know she would have had you arrested for assault! And besides if you had *bitch slapped* her and missed, I saw that fist of yours missing her and getting me and there was no way I was going to take that chance!"

Years in Puerto Vallarta and the first time I had ever thought of being physically violent with anyone. I guess problems are only opportunities in work clothes and I was equipped to do the job. My partner just looked at me and gave me a big hug and said, "I didn't know you had it in you! Thank God I just found that out now and not years ago! *You are scary*, little one!"

That evening, my angels were there giving me the courage to stand up for myself and my friend Mandi was there looking after me and protecting me from doing something I truly would have regretted later.

TODAY'S NEW FRIEND IS TOMORROW'S FAMILY

When we have lost all hope, a friend can be an angel that lifts us to our feet.

This last story is about a young man who is not so young any more. He came into my life and never left. I met Michael at a local beach bar called Montero's. It was on the beach at the end of the Malecón and four blocks down from my home. We went there often to suntan and to have a few *cervesas* or usually a bucket full of beer or two.

One late afternoon when my girlfriend Heather and I just needed to get away from it all and have a good girl to girl talk we went down to Montero's and there he was... tall and handsome with long black hair tied back against his neck with a beautiful smile and very amazing pale green eyes. Oh my god! I almost fell over; it took all I had not to stare. He came over to the table introduced himself as Michael and took our order and proceeded to talk to my friend...at that moment I knew nothing would ever come of my naughty thoughts. We might become friends, or we may not.

As time went on we talked about his life and why he spoke fluent English and his work background, where he was born and why he came back to Mexico - all these things that normally nobody cares about. I think the sharing of our lives just made us closer because most of the time people don't tell the real story of themselves and for some reason we did. We sat at the pier watching the waves roll in, looking at the surf when it hit the sandy beach then roll over the rocks that were piled up along the Malecón wall. Then we watched the sun go down as it made that hissing sound as it hit the water. We shared many, many things I don't think we ever shared with anyone else; at least I know I didn't. I told him many thoughts that I didn't share with anyone else.

Not too many people know me and what I am really all about. When I meet people for the first time, for some unknown reason they start to talk about themselves and tell me things they really shouldn't. Sometimes I feel that it was a little too much information, and many, times I have had them say, "Why did I tell you that! Please don't repeat that to anyone, please." Very rarely does anyone find out anything about me, they don't really want to know nor do they care. People are funny creatures, most of the time they are very self-centred and the quote "It's all about me" is so true. But Michael would come over to the house and I fed him and we watched TV.

Many times I would fall asleep on the chesterfield and I would wake up with a blanket on me and he would be gone. He popped in for coffee and then went to work and I would see him the next day. He never stayed overnight nor did I ever know where he lived. Funny thing is, he never told me and I never asked. He would tell me about his work night and the girls he met and for some reason they were always from England, which I thought was very strange. They were never American or Canadian girls. In time, he met my family as they can down to visit me through the years.

Michael was like the air that is around us, we don't think much about it, we take it for granted and never think of it as being very important till we can't breathe. When in fact this one element is a primary source of our existence for without it we would surely die. On an everyday basis, it's given that it should be just there for us. Air is God's gift to us and we don't even acknowledge its worth. I think looking back that's what I did with Michael. He was just there but he was truly a gift from my angels, he was my stability, my tower of strength unconsciously working in my life for many years. He was a part of my spiritual path and I think I was meant to be in his as well. In my physical world he reminded me of my dad, who I missed so much. I missed my sons as well no wonder I didn't need a man in my life, I had him.

When I started the sport bar he helped build it doing all the electrical and the plumbing and sometimes as bartender. When I look back I can remember a couple of times I was at a bar visiting the owner and he would appear out of nowhere and tell me to go home and I would just look at him and continue talking and he would stand there facing me and looking at me with that stern look and just nodding at me with that 'get out of here and go home look.' The odd part is I did! I would get up and go home and Michael would disappear and that was that. I would ask him the next day why he did that and he would say, "I didn't want anyone talking about you so I made you go before anything was to happen." I guess he knew when I was sober and when I had too much to drink and that didn't take very much – three drinks and I was on my way.

When my granddaughter got very sick and I needed to go home he went out and bought me a ticket and I just looked at him with tears in my eye. He said, "You need to go home. I will watch the bar, don't worry. Now get going and do the things you have to do before you leave." I never forgot that and I never told anyone that he had done that for me but one day I will tell my granddaughter.

I also asked him if he had sent the Shaman to see me that other day and he didn't know what I was talking about. He worked with us till I went back to Canada. Then I lost track of him. I knew he had a wife and a son. I hoped one day we would run into each other for he was definitely part of my family.

It had been a few years since I had visited Puerto Vallarta and I had lost contact with him but when I returned I ran into a friend who knew Michael and was aware that Michael was working on a project a few miles away and he would try to find him and tell him we were in town. We met up and started again like I had never been away. We were shopping for groceries the three of us. Lynda noticed and remarked, "You two are like an old married couple. You discuss everything you buy. For God's sake, it's a tomato!"

"Yeah, we are married," he remarked, "in our hearts we have been together for years."

I laughed and continued purchasing our goodies.

I wonder if a part of my spiritual awareness is my understanding of the everyday things that happen around me that I take for granted and those things are the most important and are usually the last things we look to. The repetitive acts in our world are the most important, like breathing, our heart pumping and the sun coming up every day. The wonders of the world are working in and through us all the time and I am most grateful for the miracles I don't really understand.

Angels are so much a part of my world I think they are family too.

AFTERWORD

I never realized how much the angels were working on my side, there must have been many. I know I couldn't have come this far without them.

These stories were and are about the people in my life in Puerto Vallarta that changed my way of thinking. With their love and acceptance of me I changed my attitude towards many things and recognized the inner growth I had to make to become a better person. I always questioned the fact that life had to be more than being born maybe getting married and having children, retiring, getting old then dying. *That's it?* I really didn't think so.

People come into our lives for a reason or a season or for a lifetime, some of these people make your life wonderful and others unfortunately make it just plain miserable, regardless of their role. What was mine? What was my purpose for being here on earth? Some of these people in my stories were truly angels placed in my path to help me or to make me understand something. In some cases, I was the messenger (believe me no angel) to maybe help or guide people in their paths of spiritual growth.

Unfortunately, nobody really has that answer. We have our own belief systems on what we think is going on or happening in the universal play of life. I would like to share mine.

I believe everything that is truth or principle works as one, nothing is separate from another, everything is equal for all, no exceptions to the rule. Everything is related to everything – it's how we look at it that makes it different. Science and religion are the same they just use different words for example religion says *'faith'*, science says *'confidence'*: the 'con' means 'with' ... 'fido' means 'faithful'... so we walk with faith or confidence. This gives us our ability and our need to try to reach our goals and dreams.

The word *'hope'* in religious terms takes us into the future, science says *'optimism'*. *Charity* is religious and *Love* is scientific. When they say charity begins at home they are not talking about giving things to the less fortunate they are truly talking that love does begin at home. For *Love* is the greatest of all. Nothing would exist without it. When things or people leave this earth it's because their blueprint for being here is done.

One more example, Jesus said in the eyes of god we are all equal. Well, in science we are all equal too. If we break the Law of Electricity and put our finger in an electric socket we will be electrocuted by the live current that is being generated (no choosing who will or will not be hurt – all equal). If we stand in front a moving car – rich, poor, fat, thin, old, young – we will be hit. That's the Law of Motion. No exceptions. There are many Laws and Principles that are working all the time, never-ending. The Law of Inertia keeps things operating: our heart, our eyes blinking, the sun rising every morning – they all function from this premise. In the Bible it says, "As it once was, so shall it be again." Same thing.

In my spiritual path of enlightenment I hope I can change some of my negative thoughts into positive actions that will help me and maybe others. And, when my journey comes to an end maybe I will know the reason I am here.

The end?

It's only the beginning!

CPSIA information can be obtained
at www.ICGtesting.com
Printed in the USA
LVOW12s0405210416
484588LV00001B/12/P